Praise for *Rainbow Warrior*

"The Rainbow Flag is a symbol not only of acceptance and pride but also of resilience and courage. It gives people hope, salvation, and sanctuary. Gilbert Baker gave the LGBTQ community something beautiful to stand with, something as beautiful as the community itself. *Rainbow Warrior* is his gutsy tale, a riveting and extremely moving read."

—Michael Urie, actor, director, producer

"I've always known that the Rainbow Flag was no ordinary flag, but until reading about the story behind the flag and the person behind the story, I could never have imagined the drama, conflict, creativity, and ultimately the joy behind its creation and creator. Gilbert Baker's Rainbow Flag isn't just a powerfully inspiring and unifying symbol, it also holds within its multicolored threads a gloriously rich, diverse, and often messy and contentious history of our evolving LGBTQ lives and communities."

—Eric Marcus, creator and host of the
Making Gay History podcast

"Gilbert Baker's creation of the Rainbow Flag is one of the iconic, seminal stories of our LGBTQ history. Hearing his posthumous, first-person retelling of the tale, warts and all, is a joyous and wildly entertaining thrill—and one that makes us miss him all the more."

—Bruce Cohen, Academy Award–winning producer of
Milk and *When We Rise*

"Gilbert Baker's artful memoir spools out vignettes of gay history and his own personal gay and AIDS activism in very different times, and makes them as vivid and timeless as the Rainbow Flag he created. It's a loving tribute to a successful (and colorful!) movement, and a very readable testament to how individuals can make a difference."

—Evan Wolfson, founder of Freedom to Marry

RAINBOW
WARRIOR

RAINBOW WARRIOR

MY LIFE IN COLOR

GILBERT BAKER

CHICAGO
REVIEW
PRESS

Published by Chicago Review Press Incorporated
814 North Franklin Street
Chicago, Illinois 60610
ISBN 978-1-64160-150-4

Library of Congress Cataloging-in-Publication Data
Names: Baker, Gilbert, 1951–2017, author.
Title: Rainbow warrior : my life in color / Gilbert Baker.
Description: Chicago, Illinois : Chicago Review Press, [2019]
Identifiers: LCCN 2018061304| ISBN 9781641601504 (cloth edition) | ISBN
    9781641601535 (ePub edition) | ISBN 9781641601528 (Kindle edition)
Subjects: LCSH: Baker, Gilbert, 1951–2017. | Gay activists—United
    States—Biography. | Artists—United States—Biography. | Gay liberation
    movement—United States—History. | Flags—United States—History. |
    Rainbows in art.
Classification: LCC HQ75.8.B345 B35 2019 | DDC 306.76/6092 [B] —dc23
LC record available at https://lccn.loc.gov/2018061304

Typesetting: Nord Compo

Printed in the United States of America
5 4 3 2 1

Contents

Foreword

by Dustin Lance Black

Gilbert's calls would most often come late in the evening, London time. I would already be in bed, my phone set to silent, but that wouldn't stop the screen from lighting up and pulling my eyes open. The caller ID would read the way I'd first entered his number into my phone years earlier, when we'd met on the film *Milk*: "Gilbert Rainbow." On that San Francisco morning, Gilbert had sashayed onto set with a rainbow scarf draped around his neck, cascading down his body and onto the ground below. His bejeweled jacket collar and sequined cuffs glittered in the crisp February sun. It was a spectacular morning, and he was making an undeniably spectacular entrance.

But I already knew how special Gilbert was. I knew he was the creator of the Rainbow Flag. That's why he had returned to San Francisco. We had asked him to recreate a version of his original flag for our film.

Now, years later, roused from sleep in London, I snuck out of bed so as not to wake my future husband. Once safely in our hallway, I answered the phone with a whisper: "Hello, my queen."

"Call me back, girl," he shot back, and he quickly hung up. It was only four words, but I could already hear fresh excitement in his voice, and his passion never failed to light mine up. I could tell he had just stumbled upon some new vision, and I was eager to hear it.

But calls between Harlem and London could get pricey, and though the creator of one of the most iconic symbols of the last century, Gilbert had no copyright or patent on the Rainbow Flag and thus had never reaped any seven-figure rewards for it. But, on this night, that didn't matter much. He knew full well I would gladly pay the phone bill to hear his voice.

To be clear, I'm not here to claim that there exists some sort of a gay God up in a lofty, rainbow-striped heaven, but if there was such a God, She had Gilbert Baker in first position on Her speed dial, and he spoke with Her frequently. And so, my conversations with Gilbert often felt like a three-way call with Gilbert and his heavenly gay Goddess. Most often, their visions came slowly or in pieces, and some sounded more like poetry than a plan, but on occasion an idea would emerge fully formed: aggressive, undeniable, and always dazzling.

When I got Gilbert back on the line, he asked if it was true that I would soon be traveling to Russia to screen *Milk* in a show of solidarity with Russian LGBTQ people who were in real peril thanks to Vladimir Putin's "gay propaganda" law. This law made it clear that nothing that might be interpreted as pro-LGBTQ was allowed to be seen in public. Because coming out and being visible is a necessary piece of gay liberation, and because AIDS taught us that silence and invisibility equals death, then it followed that our brothers and sisters in Russia would surely suffer under the cloak of invisibility that this new law threatened. Images of brave, bloodied Russians fighting back, many with Rainbow Flags in hand, had begun to surface on the Internet and in Western media, and with the 2014 Sochi Winter Olympics headed to Putin's shore, now was the time to shine a bright light on our brothers and sisters' plight. So yes, I told Gilbert, I was headed to Saint Petersburg and Moscow with our film.

Gilbert's voice lit up in the way that I'd come to love. I settled in on the floor to listen to him ramble out his latest design. He felt strongly that he needed to be with these Russians in some form, and so, despite his recent health struggles, he had woken up each morning over the past two weeks to turn on his sewing machine and construct a twenty-meter-long rainbow banner with the words Support Russian Gays spelled out across it in bold black letters. Now he was demanding that I bring this rainbow banner to the LGBTQ people of Russia as a show of unity and defiance.

I gave voice to what Gilbert surely already knew: that a twenty-meter-long Rainbow Flag most certainly qualified as "gay propaganda." For me to smuggle in something like that would be seen as a trespass, if not a crime. But Gilbert insisted: "They need to know we're with them. This banner will help do that. Wait until you see it. It's fabulous. They need this. We need this. And honey, you have no choice in the matter."

Only a madman might have convinced me to willfully put myself in such peril, but as it turns out, Gilbert was my favorite kind of crazy.

Gilbert's banner arrived in the mail days later. It ran the entire length of my home and back patio. It was undeniable and, as promised, truly spectacular. I quickly unloaded most of my clothes from the one carry-on bag I'd planned on taking (to insure a speedy exit if necessary), and I jammed Gilbert's goliath roll of gay propaganda deep into the bottom of it. Then, based on a tip from a local, I paid the Russian airline's "VIP travel fee" in hopes that their VIP security might be willing to turn a blind eye. A day later, I made it into Saint Petersburg with little more than a cross look from the airport's VIP customs agent. I could almost hear Gilbert's voice in my ear: "You go, girl."

That night, our *Milk* screening was interrupted three times by bomb threats. Each time, everyone in the theater was forced to shuffle out into the snow and bear the taunts and threats from a gaggle of homophobes dressed in black for the hour it took Russian police to check the theater for explosives. But each time we were allowed back in, it became clear that in the face of such threats, more and more LGBTQ Russians were showing up. By the end of that night, the theater was jammed.

When I finally unfurled Gilbert's rainbow creation, it proved long enough to wrap around the room, and around all of us, Americans and Russians alike. As Gilbert had promised, we did feel like one family in that moment, and these LGBTQ Russians were visibly emboldened by Gilbert's offering. For years to come, I saw photos of that banner being marched down Russian streets, held aloft by lines of brave freedom fighters being greeted by fists, Tasers, clubs, and worse—but knowing full well that they were not alone in their struggle. Nearly forty years after its creation, Gilbert and his flag had once again proven their power and worth.

After my return from Russia, Gilbert began calling more often, and even later into the night. His direct line to that gay God seemed more active than ever, and his calls were now laser focused on sourcing the practical bits that visionaries always need but too often struggle to nail down: finances, materials, contacts, and collaborators. Night after night, his notions and new ideas grew—multiplying and magnifying as they flew across the ocean and into my ear.

"A video installation piece inside of San Francisco Airport. The flag will be a part of it. But it must go beyond that, girl. It has to wrap itself around every traveler. They will all *be* it. In it. They will see themselves in all of us," he whispered to me one night. The next week it was this very book he wanted to discuss. "I started writing it over a decade ago. But it wasn't its time. *Now* is the time. It's time to share the full story of the Rainbow Flag's creation with the world . . . so that the world knows how it came to be, so that it can keep growing—shifting and growing."

History buff that I am, I began asking him about its past, but he pushed back, insisting the rainbow's story reach further forward than backward, and then, using his trademark expansive, transformative language, he described the flag's future: never fixed, always finding new stages, forms, and family members. I would sit in the dark and listen to him for an hour or more. Because, beyond the flag itself, this was Gilbert's great gift: his visionary voice. For me, it was hypnotic and damn addictive.

Through these late-night conversations, I came to see Gilbert's flag not as a singular object but as an embrace, one he was abidingly certain had the potential to expand indefinitely—to include future generations, any current event or ongoing social justice struggle, and all of the yet-to-be-examined variations of our diverse LGBTQ family. I came to understand that Gilbert's flag wasn't meant to be static, because an embrace is not a static thing—it must shift and adapt to the needs of time and place. And, of course, it must continue to grow, because as long as the Rainbow Flag stands for acceptance, justice, and equality for all, it has to keep expanding.

The last time I saw Gilbert was at a New York screening of *When We Rise*, a TV series that depicts a sliver of the story of the birth of his Rainbow Flag, sending two Gilbert-dyed-and-sewn recreations of his flags up the same poles at United Nations Plaza in San Francisco from which the originals had first flown. Afterward, he came up to me with tears in his eyes, looked deep into mine, and said "Thank you" three times. I had never seen Gilbert cry like this before. I could feel something in him changing, but I didn't know what yet. His wet eyes that night haunted me.

Not long after that, I was walking home from a late-night dinner in London, and my phone rang. This time the call was from Cleve Jones, Gilbert's longtime friend and activist coconspirator. "Gilbert's gone," Cleve told me. It was impossible to believe, but true. Somewhere in the night, without warning, that gay God had come for our great visionary. Gilbert was no longer on our earth.

Over the next few weeks, I tried my best to find silver linings in all of the Rainbow Flags hanging outside of businesses, the stickers in windows and on cars, or the entire buses covered in his rainbow creation. And although each rainbow made the monumental success of his life's work evident, no number of Rainbow Flags could fill the void his passing left. I was heartbroken. I would never again find myself sitting in my underwear in a dark hallway listening to his glittering voice from across an ocean. Or so I thought.

Nearly two years later, I woke up to a message from Gilbert's dear friend Charley Beal. Charley let me know that he had found various versions of Gilbert's long-simmering memoir, many chapters written decades apart, and that he had helped piece them together as best he could. He'd found a publisher, an editor, and now it seemed that Gilbert's story, in his own words, was ready to meet the world. I told Charley I had to read it immediately. As luck would have it, the manuscript landed in my inbox at night. I once again snuck out of bed, into the hall, and read it from beginning to end.

There he was. There was our magnificent Gilbert. I could hear his dazzling, dreamy voice again, not just from across an ocean but from the great beyond—from that rainbow-striped heaven I feel certain he feels quite at home in now.

These pages hold Gilbert's joy—his visions, untamed spirit, flashes of unbridled bitchiness, and all of the unvarnished truths of who he and his collaborators were and are. These pages share his moments of towering confidence, his vast periods of great doubt, his tireless search for accomplices to help realize his impossible dreams, and those few moments of success that made all the suffering worthwhile. This book tells the story of an artist and an activist's unyielding, lifelong dedication to a singular creative notion, and his courage to let that creation go, to let it be shared, to let it bend and find new forms in order for it to remain timeless, boundless, and ever inclusive of our growing LGBTQ family. These pages are now the worthy home of this exceedingly rare, once-in-a-generation, irrepressible voice. So kick off your shoes—hell, strip down to your underwear—find a darkened hallway, and let his voice show you how the impossible might come to be.

Dustin Lance Black *is an Academy Award–winning filmmaker and social activist, best known for his film and TV work including* Milk, J. Edgar, *and* When We Rise, *and for his memoir* Mama's Boy. *Black was also a founding board member of the American Foundation for Equal Rights, which successfully led the California and Virginia federal cases for marriage equality, putting an end to California's discriminatory Proposition 8.*

RAINBOW
WARRIOR

Flags are torn from the soul of the people.
I created the Rainbow Flag in 1978.
It evolved to become the international symbol
for the gay, lesbian, bisexual, and transgender movement.
This is the story of how it happened.
—GB, 1996

1

A Bolt of Lightning

On June 25, 1978, San Francisco awoke to a cool morning with sharp, clear skies. I watched the sunrise with my friends Faerie and James through the windows of the Gay Community Center, a block away from city hall. We had been up all night, driven by the exuberance that comes with youth and heightened expectation, lovingly putting the final touches on my creation: the Rainbow Flag.

I was twenty-seven. I loved to sew and imagined myself an artist. The idea for the Rainbow Flag had come to me in a dance to a tribal beat, on the wings of angels. Infused with the colors of God's covenant with humanity, the Rainbow Flag was more than mere cloth; it was a visual metaphor and an active proclamation of power, created and dedicated to gay and lesbian liberation. It declared that sexuality is a beautiful expression of nature, a human right.

The weather felt more than perfect that morning. I was floating on adrenaline as we headed to the place designated for the birth of the Rainbow Flag: San Francisco's United Nations Plaza. The site was crowned by two flagpoles eight stories high and a hundred feet apart. These slender sentinel towers of bronze and steel symbolically formed a colossal ceremonial entrance gate from Market Street to the Civic Center and the broad plaza beyond, extending all the way to city hall.

On each tall flagpole, we attached a thirty-by-sixty-foot flag. We paused once in our ritual to offer one final embrace of the carefully folded bundles. Then we raised them and they ascended like sails. As they unfurled, a Pacific zephyr suddenly whipped up, powered by invisible ancestors, and pulled the flags from our arms into God's. The twin Rainbow Flags were now as uncontrollable as the forces of nature that pushed them up into the sky.

At that moment, life breathed the song of the Great Spirit into the flags. For a second, frozen in time, we flew high with it, our hearts blowing glorious trumpets of beautiful joy. Their first moments of flight were astonishing to behold: The wind-painted colors in explosive motion, a wild flame-like flickering, a magical, rippling, psychedelic, cotton-aerial dance.

The few people at United Nations Plaza who witnessed its birth were now staring up with wonder at the fruits of our long labor. They were getting it, owning it, feeling it as a part of them, understanding the diversity of sexual freedom it represented for everyone: gay, lesbian, bisexual, transgender, straight, whatever your sex, whatever your color. *Visible*, with liberty and justice for all.

That moment felt like a bolt of lightning that I surely knew would change the course of my life. What I didn't know at the time was how the Rainbow Flag would change the world.

2

Dreaming of a Life
Over the Rainbow

When people find out I'm from Kansas, they often ask me, jokingly, "Oh, are you a friend of Dorothy?" I always tell them, "I *am* Dorothy."

My father, Lyle Phillip Baker, was from Johnson City, Kansas. He was born August 31, 1929. My mother, Patricia Lou Carson, was born July 10, 1932, in Chanute, where my parents were married in 1950. I was born there at Neosho Memorial Hospital on June 2, 1951.

I was born gay and I always knew it.

I was a smart child, and my parents were thrilled when I learned to read and write before I even started school. But by the time I was in kindergarten, I had also developed a drag routine. In my bedroom, when no one was looking, I would pull the sheet from my bed and wrap it around me, then tie the pastel percale all different ways and play with the soft fabric billows. (Even then, fabric fascinated me; whenever I touched it, I went to another place, a nirvana.) Then, wrapped in my colorful bedsheet, I would dance to the radio. When I heard someone coming, I would quickly put the sheet back on the bed—putting my secret life back in my mind's box.

Then one day, I discovered my aunt's old prom dress in a hall closet outside my bedroom. Excited by my find, I waited until everybody was out of the house so I could try it on and dance around and around like a grand lady. I did it again and again. But one day, while I whirled and twirled, my parents came home unexpectedly and caught me in the act.

My father spanked me and scolded me, saying, "Stop acting like a girl."

After that day, my mom and dad would yell at me whenever I acted out in a feminine way, asking me, "Why can't you just be normal?"

But I didn't stop. Instead, I led a double life, one on the outside and one on the inside. That strategy might have worked, but I was far too wild a child, a free spirit compelled by nature to fly into the freedom of my imagination. When I was alone, I didn't have to act like a boy, however a boy was supposed to act. I wondered if that was because I was really a girl. If I was a girl, then why wasn't I born that way?

I had been baptized in a Methodist church. I believed in God, read the Bible, recited the Lord's Prayer, and went to Sunday school. But in my soul, questions burned: Did God make me gay and love me, or was I going to hell for a sin?

All those around me thought I was hopeless, my fate predestined. Alone in my childhood spiritual crisis, I crawled under my bedroom covers, considering ways to commit suicide. I had heard of ways to do it. But I feared the pain of using a razor blade or the difficulty of swallowing pills. So I pushed those plans aside. Somehow, I learned to cope with the pain of rejection and the shame of failure that filled my childhood and teen years. But the dark thoughts of taking my own life never ever left me. From time to time, alone at night, I would return to that lonely, hopeless place, and pray that God would take me back. And when he didn't answer my prayers, I would fall asleep and dream of a life somewhere over the rainbow.

But while I coped with the terror of feeling mentally deformed, I had another, more obvious problem: I had only one testicle. The other had never descended and was still tucked up in my stomach. Physically, then, I was also a freak. Mom and Dad eventually told me that it could all be corrected with surgery and I'd be just like all the other boys. But I knew that other boys didn't dress up in their aunt's prom dress. Would that operation fix everything about me?

———————

By the time I was five, two sisters had joined our family. Gail was two by then, and my younger sister Ardonna was a toddler. We had moved to Topeka, where my father was attending law school. We lived in army buildings that had been turned into student housing for veterans on the GI Bill. My mother worked part time at a local five-and-dime store. The previous Christmas, she'd bought us our first television.

In 1956, not every family had a TV. So the house filled up with neighbors when something important was on, like the Democratic or Republican National Convention. President Eisenhower was from Kansas and he was running for his second term, so my mother let me watch these political events with the grown-ups. I was mesmerized by the hoopla of bunting and balloons and thrilled by the pageantry. I especially loved the parade of state delegates, each group carrying signs and banners created in crepe paper. There were crazy hats and pretty girls in sashes of stars and stripes, the national anthem and the Pledge of Allegiance. I was especially moved by the sight of the American flag.

Inspired by the patriotic beauty of the conventions, I devoted myself to drawing crayon pictures of what I had seen. Then I became fascinated with the Miss America pageant, which was just starting to be televised. I loved designing elaborate ball gowns for Lee Meriwether, Miss America 1955. She was the most beautiful person I'd ever seen. What I wanted most for my birthday was a strapless ball gown in taffeta and tulle.

But this, after all, was Kansas in 1956. It was not considered normal to imagine greatness and beauty. Being an artist was bad in the same way that homosexuality was bad. Anyone who took up that kind of career was a sexual suspect. When I first told my parents that I wanted to be an artist, they responded in extremely negative terms. It was as if I had told them I was also gay. (And maybe in a way I had.) So while I was obviously talented with my hands and had a strong visual sense, there was not much hope for me becoming a fashion designer or a painter. Dad and Mom had a solution—or, rather, a distraction: instead of a gown for my birthday, they gave me an Erector Set (manufactured, ironically, by the Gilbert toy company) to channel my creativity into more masculine areas.

Eventually, my father started his own law practice and we moved to the big city of Wichita. I did well in my new school, but my imagination and dreams took me to other worlds far away. By the time I was nine, I needed to know more about myself and my "condition." I went to the local library and found a book about Freud and abnormal psychology. It explained the concept of "delusions of grandeur." I convinced myself that I was the one Freud was writing about. I started to wonder if I might be mentally ill. This idea that I might be psychotic made me afraid that my parents would send me to a mental institution. I struggled to tone down my behavior and pretended to be interested in girls. But I was consumed by the weight of the lies that I told every day just to survive. So I acted as if everything in my waking life conformed to the ordinary. To keep my parents' love, I pretended to be someone I wasn't.

In fifth grade, I finally had the operation on my testicle. I woke up in St. Joseph's Hospital with steel sutures holding my gut together. An elastic string was taped to my knee. It was attached through my scrotum to my newly lowered testicle to keep it in place. The nurses gave me morphine at first, and then some pills. But I was black and blue for two months and could barely walk. People now had another reason to laugh at me.

Eventually, the stitches came out and I was given the all clear on the male apparatus. But my hope that the operation would be successful on all parts of me was dashed. I hadn't been cured; I still wanted to sketch fashion, create art, and dance around in dresses. I was still different, not like all the other boys at all.

I finally got up my nerve and went back to the library. Deep in the back of the stacks, I took out the same book that explained Freud and abnormal psychology. I read further and began learning about homosexuality. I knew I was one of them too, and I wanted to know more.

I now had a name to explain why I felt the way I did. My parents had told me for years, "We're all just plain people, no different from anyone else." But I wasn't like them or anyone I knew. I felt so alien that I wondered if I had been adopted. I was a homosexual. I wanted to be an artist. I wanted to be famous. I wanted to live in Paris, not Wichita. I hated my life.

But then a miracle happened that lifted my spirits and gave me hope. I entered a school art contest and won a scholarship to an art academy in the old part of Wichita. Resigned that I was never going to be a doctor or engineer, my parents finally relented. On Saturdays, my mother would drive me there for the classes that were held in a rundown, 1920s Italianate mansion. I loved the homes in the area; each featured a different style of architecture, and all of them were beautifully laid out, one after another, on spacious lots connected by broad, tree-lined streets. They looked so different from where we lived. In my neighborhood, the new part of town, there weren't any trees and all the tract houses looked the same.

The art academy had turned the first floor of the mansion into a gallery. Paintings and sculptures of naked people were on display. I was fascinated with the male nudes. It turned me on to look at them. Secretly, I began to draw little abstract versions of penises and testicles. I knew what they were, but my classmates just looked at them blankly.

―――――――――

A few miles away from our house, on the outskirts of town, was the Boeing aircraft factory where they made B-52 bombers. The US government had also initiated plans to surround Wichita with missile sites. The missiles were designed to launch in retaliation when the inevitable Russian attack happened. One crisp October afternoon when I was eleven, we were all sent home from school early. My parents and some neighbors were sitting tensely in front of the television, listening to President Kennedy announce some kind of war with Cuba. He talked of Russian missiles that were placed in formation to hit every town in

America. The Boeing facility in our own city of Wichita was named as a primary target of the Russian missiles.

As the dramatic events of the Cuban Missile Crisis unfolded, we stayed glued to the television. Reports from Washington offered terrifying instructions on what to do in the event of an atomic war. My family discussed how we would jump into action to save ourselves. Dad created a plan that we rehearsed over and over again: When the sirens went off, we were supposed to run directly home from school. All five of us—Dad, Mom, me, Gail, and Ardonna—would get into my mother's 1955 Chevy sedan. I would make sure we brought along my dog Bruiser, a large AKC brindle boxer. We would get out of town on the back roads and drive all the way to the Oklahoma Panhandle to be with relatives in Enid. (That area was not a Russian target, we were told.) That's as far as the plan went; it wasn't clear what would happen after that. But I felt confident that Bruiser and the bow-and-arrow set that I got for Christmas would protect me from the hydrogen bomb.

For many years afterward, I would have recurring dreams in which the government would alert us of impending doom and urge us to evacuate. After a long and arduous escape from Wichita to Enid, we suddenly would be blown up in a nuclear mushroom cloud. I would die in a terrible flash of light, holding my beloved Bruiser.

About a year later, I was in seventh-grade gym class. The period was almost over and the instructor had sent us to the locker room for showers. I hated gym class, and I was always afraid I would get a hard-on in the showers in front of the other boys. I was discreetly drying myself off when an announcement came over the intercom, telling us all to proceed to our next class—there was an emergency. Over a classmate's transistor radio, I learned that President Kennedy had been shot in Dallas.

Not too much later, another announcement came: President Kennedy was dead. School was suspended for the rest of the day. I went home and sat with the family in front of the television. In a trance, I watched the coverage nonstop until the next morning. Kansas was a bastion of the Republican Party, so many people took the shooting in stride, as if it was destined. Kennedy was a Catholic, and there was something about him that went against the Kansas grain.

That Sunday, we traveled to my grandparents' house in Chanute, about a hundred miles east of Wichita. Around noon, all the relatives gathered in the dining room for prayer before the meal. My uncle Dale, the most devout, called everyone to silence. There was a national crisis going on, he said, and this moment was going to bring us all together. He began to say grace. In the living room, the black-and-white television was still on, broadcasting the news from Dallas. Kennedy's assassin was being transferred to the county jail. I hoped that the prayer wouldn't go on too long, because I wanted to get back to the tube. As we all bowed our heads, I turned in time to watch as Jack Ruby shot Lee Harvey Oswald. Everyone heard the shot and gasped, and suddenly my parents and aunts and uncles all began reciting the Lord's Prayer.

The next day, Kennedy's funeral was on TV, and it was riveting. Never had I seen such incredible pageantry and solemn rituals acted out. Later, when everything had reached a numb plateau, I would run off into the woods near our house. I would dress up like Jackie Kennedy and pretend to light the eternal flame at the grave of the dead young president.

Death became my obsession. Only one thing seemed certain about my life in Kansas: I would either be blown up by a nuclear bomb or die from boredom. One day, I found a book of cartoons by Charles Addams featuring his creations the Addams Family. I wanted to live like they did, with everyone dressed in black and weird looking. *Mad* magazine was another favorite. Satire became an acceptable forum for my anger. My own drawings soon reflected my darkening mood.

I went to school and continued studying art. Everything else I learned from the television. One night I was watching *The Tonight Show*. One of the guests was a hilarious woman named Phyllis Diller. She dressed outrageously and had a long cigarette holder like a whacked-out Cruella de Vil. Her jokes were all about her husband Fang, the squalid, meaningless lives they lived, and their attempts to put on airs and conform to the all-American, suburban status quo. It was, I realized, a satire of my own family's striving middle-class background. Phyllis Diller has always been one of my idols, because she reinvented herself as the original acid-trip housewife.

But my favorite TV star was Barbra Streisand. She was "it" because her talent and voice were so passionate, so political. People either loved her or hated her. Barbra was different and she owned it. She wouldn't get her nose fixed, and she was so Jewish, a beatnik, kooky. When she sang, it was like hearing a secret part of my life expressed. She connected gay people to one another—if you liked her, it was like a code. She was so much cooler than Judy Garland, who had been the great gay diva until then. Even though they sang the same type of songs, there was a difference between the two: Judy was the victim; Barbra was the warrior.

I became more and more interested in music. It dominated the culture of the '60s, even in Kansas. My grandmother played a good boogie-woogie on the piano, but I wanted to be in a band. The Beatles and the Rolling Stones were becoming popular. At first, it was all about their long-hair mop-tops. Old people said that they looked like girls, so they were definitely pushing a button on the taboo of homosexuality. The Stones in particular flaunted themselves as decadent dandies.

Luckily, my family and teachers were more receptive to my musical aspirations than my artistic ones. I got a cornet and practiced every day. After a couple of months, I traded up for a trumpet, which I liked better. Music became my means of survival all through my teenage years. It was the way I could compensate socially for being so effeminate and being known as the class queer. As long as I was playing my trumpet, no one would bother me. Bruiser would sit at my feet and howl to the moon as I tooted up and down the scales and learned every Burt Bacharach song.

I played in the marching band in high school and I was good at it, though I sometimes fantasized about being a drum major or baton twirler. The music revolution was happening. We didn't want to play Sousa marches; we wanted numbers by Herb Alpert & the Tijuana Brass and Blood, Sweat & Tears. I pushed teachers to include contemporary music in our band programs. My efforts succeeded, and I even became popular with my classmates because of it.

But the real turning point in my youth was the 1968 Democratic National Convention. The Vietnam War was something we had watched every night on the news, but that year there was an explosion of anti-war protest. After the assassinations of Martin Luther King and Robert Kennedy, the Chicago convention became the battleground for a clash between the two Americas. One was over thirty and not to be trusted. The other was mad as hell and in the streets. But the only thing taking over the streets in Kansas was tumbleweed.

I sat on the sofa, glued to the convention coverage. Chicago looked like another country. Once in a while, a reporter would interview one of the student leaders about their protests. "Dirty hippies, commies, revolutionaries, queers . . ." the neighbors in my house would say whenever one of the kids spoke out. I listened to the war of words that brought the generation gap right into my own living room. Ugly confrontations between me and my parents started to occur with regularity. I was nineteen by then, and I knew it was finally time for me to leave home.

So, unlike Dorothy, when the tornado came I ran right for it, saying, "Take me away!"

3

I Am Not a Homosexual

Getting out of Kansas was my dream. Being an artist—and being gay—was not safe there. If I couldn't escape, I knew I would end up a suicide. On my nineteenth birthday, in June 1970, I was drafted into the army. I wanted to go. I would serve two years and see the world. I would be an adventurer and traveler.

During the induction process, I was shown into a little cubicle. Inside was a small desk presided over by a sergeant. He began to ask questions about my personal history, making notes on a form. Eventually, he came to the part I had dreaded. He looked directly at me and asked, "Are you a homosexual?"

"No," I responded. I had told the same lie for years; it felt natural.

"Are you sure?" he said. He didn't believe me. "You sound like one."

Whenever I tried to pass as straight, my voice was my downfall. "I have a cold," I explained.

He looked at me with great intensity, as if he could see through me. The sergeant's face showed he still wasn't convinced.

I said it again in a deeper voice. "I am not a homosexual."

"You talking to me?" he asked, his voice rising in anger. "Always address me as 'sir.'"

"I am not a homosexual, sir!" I put the emphasis on every word. He still wasn't buying it.

I thought of the consequences of being turned away for being queer. My family would have me committed to a mental institution. I'd be given electroshock therapy. I was scared. This guy had my future in his hands.

"Well, have you ever had a homosexual experience?" the sergeant continued.

I shook my head.

"Do you know it's a felony crime to lie in these proceedings? If we find out you lied about this matter, we can send you to the penitentiary and you will get a dishonorable discharge. Do you know what that means?"

I didn't know and I kept my mouth shut.

He explained the process of being dishonorably discharged, and the stigma attached to it, adding, "It means your life won't be worth shit."

He was challenging me to speak up.

"The army is no place for a queer. You look like a sissy to me," he prodded again.

I stayed mute.

But I knew I was a homosexual. Every waking moment was given over to erotic fantasies. I was never interested in girls, and always afraid of boys. The truth haunted me. Everything in the outside world said that this is wrong, that I was damned. Inside, every hormone screamed that this "love that dare not speak its name" was so right.

He finally gave up and signed off on the bottom of my form. "Don't say I didn't warn you."

I was sent down the hall for my physical exam. There, I lined up with fellow recruits and we took our clothes off. In a room full of naked men, I prayed I wouldn't get a hard-on. A doctor came in, put on rubber gloves, and told us to stand against the wall. He went from one guy to the next, first listening to our hearts with a stethoscope and then holding our testicles while he made us cough. I was the last in line.

He put the cold metal disk on my chest and listened. I was so nervous, I thought my heart might stop beating. He moved it here and there, checking and rechecking. Being turned away for a weak heart would have been more acceptable than being labeled a homosexual, I thought. It would make a lifetime of explanation easier.

The physician then put his hand under my balls. "Turn your head and cough." I did. He gave a little laugh. "Hernia?" he asked. Everyone turned to look. Time froze. Embarrassed, I stared straight ahead, explaining, "It was fixed when I was twelve." The doctor kept his hands on my testicles, rolling them through his fingers. I could feel a drop of sweat begin its descent down my nose.

At last it was over. We dressed and were told to report to the commanding officer. I entered a room full of Sears plywood paneling, dominated by an American flag. Together, we recited the Pledge of Allegiance. Then we were asked to recite the army oath, declaring that we were ready to die for our country. A new life was underway; I was now Private Baker.

Carrying overnight bags, we boarded a Greyhound bus. In a state of terrified curiosity, I stayed awake all night, watching the countryside speed past, as the bus drove east toward Missouri. Fort Leonard Wood was where we would undergo basic training. This trial by fire would turn us into men, according to sacred military myth. Serving one's country in the armed forces was guaranteed to make a real man out of anyone, even a queer. Secretly, I hoped it was true.

I wasn't obsessed with being normal, but I could see the advantages of not being a sexual suspect—or in my case, a sexual certainty. You didn't get hassled if you passed; you were part of the club. The ideology of masculinity formed the basis of your identity. Life was easy street if you were straight. I lived a lie.

All the buses pulled up to the gates of Fort Leonard Wood, one after another, delivering their human cargo. I saw morning dew steaming from a big fence and from an even bigger American flag. I could hear a voice inside my mind, telling me that I was making a mistake.

We disembarked single file. Immediately, there were people telling you what to do. Go here. Stand there. And there were other people telling them what to do. Voices stacked on top of each other until a huge white noise filled my ears. There were thousands of us. I could barely absorb the terrible spectacle of it and kept my eyes to the ground.

We were instructed to climb onto cattle cars in a train that took us to another part of the fort. There we were given crew cuts and issued uniforms and equipment. We stood in more lines as our names were called out yet again, and we were assembled into battalions. Then we were divided into companies and finally platoons. We stood for hours on the hot railway platform, dressed in heavy wool clothing and helmets. It was nearly a hundred degrees. Each of us carried ninety-pound duffel bags. We were hustled onto another train. Some soldiers had to run and jump. "Move it! Move it!" the officers barked in our faces. I moved it and we moved out. They left all the doors on the train open. To relieve the suffering in the heat, I drank from my canteen.

The train chugged its way into a big compound of four-story, brown-brick barracks, laid out in an orderly campus. I was one of more than ten thousand men assigned for the current cycle of instruction. We were met at the dock by the drill sergeant to whom we would answer. Besides drill sergeants, there were more sergeants, lieutenants, and captains who arranged our whole group in rectangles of humanity. We were told to run to a big assembly area between the brick dormitories. We stood on the concrete, silent and at attention in neat rows. The midday sun burned down.

The drill sergeant walked up and down the line and told us how to stand: straighten up here, shoulders back, eyes forward. He barked out our names, reading them from our uniforms. He checked our dog tags and made marks on a clipboard. You could not stand at ease until he had signed you off. As I waited my turn, I felt weak, sweating and trembling under the heavy load of the duffel bag on my shoulder. Suddenly, I fell to the ground in a haze of exploding stars before my eyes.

"You fucking faggot. You pansy," the drill sergeant was saying, his face in mine, administering blasts of amyl nitrite to revive me. He hauled me to my feet and marched me to the front of the formation. I was in trouble. I faced him while he spoke over my shoulder, addressing everyone behind me. "This queer is a piece of shit, a turd," he sneered.

"That's what you are, Baker. That's your name." Suddenly a lieutenant was standing in front of me, his West Point eyes boring a hole through my head. "What's the problem, Baker?"

The drill sergeant answered: "He's a fag."

The lieutenant looked closer at me. "Are you a fag, Baker?"

"No," I said, my head still spinning.

"No, what?" the drill sergeant screamed, because I had forgotten to say "sir" again. He shook my shoulders. "You turd, get down on the ground and give me twenty." He pushed me to the burning concrete.

My feeble strength made it hard to lower myself to the ground and then push myself up. I thought I might pass out again, as the drill sergeant barked out, "One, two, three . . ."

"This turd is a queer," the drill sergeant repeated to the lieutenant matter-of-factly. "The little girl can't even do a push-up."

The lieutenant called the company to attention. Everyone would do push-ups. They would do them until I had done twenty. It was a moment in hell. One by one, the other drill sergeants all came to the front of the formation to see the cause of this disciplinary action. "Fucking queer," some of them spat out, doing so with such anger I wondered if they might kill me on the spot. They kicked their boots under my face and spat on me. Then they joined in sounding off the count. The lieutenant addressed the groveling multitude, explaining how everyone was paying in punitive push-ups for this queer's sin. A sin against masculinity.

They say looks can kill. It seemed possible that afternoon, when faced with a thousand angry stares from the other recruits. Everyone hated me.

From reveille to lights out, I lived in terror. At any moment, I could be called forward again and verbally beaten in front of the entire company. Guys were threatening me. Sometimes, I was too afraid to sleep. I knew I was in over my head.

There were the rare bright spots. One day, we were all taken to the arsenal for weapons training and issued M16s. We had to take them apart and reassemble them. Unexpectedly, luck smiled on me; I was the first to complete the complicated task. More than once. Of course, the victory was short lived; the sergeant would march us off afterward, double-time, for ten miles.

The worst was the firing range. Target practice pushed me over the edge. We were forced to put on headphones and lie down in a bed of gravel. I held the M16 cradled against my shoulder with my finger on the trigger. There were small tin cartridges full of bullets. I fed them in ten at a time. When we were given the command to fire, cardboard targets in the shape of bodies sprung up a hundred yards across a dusty field. I closed my eyes and squeezed the metal trigger.

"You're a turd, Baker." The drill sergeant was suddenly right on top of me. "I want you to see what happens to queers who can't shoot."

The drill sergeant halted the proceedings and walked out to the black-and-white targets. My target, he announced, didn't have any bullet holes. He reached down and lifted up a watermelon and set it on the target area. He strutted back to me, grabbed my gun, and began firing round after round into the melon. The fruit exploded, blood-red chunks flying everywhere. Triumphantly, he announced, "That, everyone, is what happens to queers and gooks."

"Gooks" was what they called the North Vietnamese. He was saying I was the enemy. He leaned closer to me and added, "Queers die." I felt vomit blister up the back of my throat. He ordered push-ups for everyone else until I hit the target.

The next day, I was called out of the chow line and summoned to where the drill sergeants were having their meal. They amused themselves by making up names for me and placing bets on how long I would live. They concluded that I wouldn't even make it to 'Nam. Maybe someone would just shoot me during basic training.

One of the drill sergeants asked me, "Do you want to die?"

"No," I managed to get out of my mouth. They howled with laughter.

"A turd like you wants to live. That's the funniest thing."

One of the drill sergeants took off his hat, wiped sweat from his face, and extended his wet hand. "Thirsty?" he asked. The others went into hysterics. I looked into the face of evil. He pulled a pistol from his belt and waved it in front of me. "I wouldn't let a queer turd suck my dick," he growled, firing the pistol in the air like a cowboy. I jumped.

I decided to get out of the army. I made a plan. I wasn't going to carry a weapon. I would identify as a conscientious objector.

Morning came and we made our way to the aluminum-and-steel arsenal building for M16s for the day's march to the firing range. We were going on a three-day bivouac. I fumbled for a semiautomatic from a long row of rifles. As the company commanders called to move out, at the last moment I didn't pick up the gun. Instead, I took my place in the formation, the next to last row.

We marched forward from the barracks singing little ditties that soldiers chant. After a few minutes, the guys immediately next to me whispered, "Where's your weapon?"

"I'm not going to use it," I nervously replied. I wondered if they would tell the sergeant and have me busted. But they just minded their own business, knowing this was sure to be big trouble.

We marched and double-timed our way into the Missouri countryside a few miles. It was a hot summer day. Flies and locusts buzzed around us. An hour passed, and I was amazed no one had said anything. Then, as we were jogging, I noticed the drill sergeant fix on me, fall back, and run alongside of me. He stared in surprise, making sure that what his eyes told him was true.

"You don't have a weapon, Baker." I didn't speak and kept my eyes forward. "You fuckup," he added, in a tone that let me know I was in for it. The drill sergeant went up front in the direction of the big brass. As we were coming down a hillside, I could see them conferring several hundred yards ahead. Whistles suddenly blew the march to a stop. A jeep was coming back in my direction, carrying the drill sergeant and the officer of the day.

"Baker, where is your weapon?" the officer asked.

"I didn't pick it up this morning."

"Did you forget your weapon, Gomer?" the captain said, referring to a dimwitted TV character in the marines.

"I will not carry a weapon," I announced with nervous resolve. "I want to file for discharge as a conscientious objector." My words blew up with the force of a bomb.

"Get down on the ground," the captain screamed. "I don't want to see your face! You make me puke." I fell into the dust.

"Everyone will do push-ups until you go back and get your weapon!" I could hear the groans of several thousand men.

I looked up from my prone position right into his face. "You can do what you want, but I'm not going to carry a gun. I have the right to file for discharge as a conscien—"

"You haven't got shit for rights!" the captain screamed. He pulled me up by the neck, shouting, "You better wake up, fucker, if you know what's good for you!" I said nothing. A drill sergeant approached and reported that a call had already gone to the colonel and the base commander was on his way. As we waited for his arrival, I watched a carpet of heaving bodies pushing up and down in the dirt.

The colonel drove up in a jeep with flags on the fenders. "You're a coward," was all he said. The captain and the others waited for him to render a decision about what to do with me. He discussed it with several of the other officers and decided his verdict was treason.

The officer of the day, his hand on the pistol in his holster, approached me. "We could kill you on the spot," he told me. "We would have every right to shoot you as a deserter. Nobody would think twice about a dead queer. What do you think about that, Baker?"

"I think that would be murder," I said in a hoarse whisper. He was scaring me.

Instead of execution, I was driven back to the barracks by military police. I was told to speak to no one until the officer of the day came for me. They posted a guard at the door of my bunk.

Two hours later, a staff sergeant walked in. He carried a manila envelope. It was full of forms that I would have to fill out to begin the process of being discharged as a conscientious objector. "Get these back to me first thing in the morning," he said, tossing the pile of paperwork on my bunk.

I was given permission to make phone calls. My parents were outraged and made it clear that they would never support my decision. Conscientious objectors were all cowards and deserters. I would be the shame of the entire family.

A maelstrom of emotion had me in its grip when I walked into the staff sergeant's office with a sheaf of incomplete forms. I knew my bid for discharge would be denied. "Well, Baker, it seems to me you've got a problem," he said, as he glanced through the paperwork. "But maybe we can work something out."

I was astonished. It was the first time anyone had addressed me with the slightest tinge of humanity since my induction. "You say here you don't want to carry a weapon for moral reasons," he said, pondering a moment before he added, "Why don't you put in for medic? Under the Geneva Convention, medics do not have to carry guns. I can fix it, and all this trouble will be out of my hair. You'll get out of here alive and you can get an honorable discharge. Otherwise, your case is going nowhere and you'll be kept here in basic training until they decide what to do with you."

I knew the part about the Geneva Convention was bullshit, but I accepted. Word went out that I was being assigned to the medic corps. As I spent my last weeks in basic training, I was hounded with tales of a gruesome ending for any medic in Vietnam. In addition, I was terrified to the last moment that they would call off the deal before I got on a plane to San Antonio.

"Army personnel," as medics were now referred to, were required to receive job training. San Antonio was the site of Brooks Army Medical Center and the medic training program. Instead of shooting M16s, my colleagues and I spent our days in classrooms. I excelled on most of the endless tests. At the end of the instruction, I was offered a chance to become a nurse. All I had to do was serve out a two-year enlistment. I accepted.

Instead of Vietnam, I would be sent to San Francisco.

4

A Door Opens

When I got to San Francisco, I knew I wasn't ever going back to Kansas. I was assigned to barracks built on the sandy shores of the bay. My cubicle had a window with an unobstructed view of the Golden Gate Bridge. There was a period of downtime before the next nursing class would convene. I was given a temporary job, three days a week, at the Oakland army depot.

Thursday through Monday, I was in the army. My job was to collect urine and blood samples from troops returning from Vietnam and test them for venereal disease and drugs. I worked long hours. Every day, thousands of men came through the huge processing center. These guys were headed home. There was a communication going on among these Vietnam veterans that those of us stateside could not understand. I just did my job and tried not to think about the war going on.

On my days off from blood and urine testing, I explored San Francisco with another soldier. Jim was a miniature Rhett Butler, all deep southern accent. We were assigned to the same nursing program, lived in the same barracks, and worked at the same job in Oakland. He soon became my best friend.

October in San Francisco is an Indian summer. At that time of year, it is surely the most beautiful city in the world. Jim and I would walk across the Golden Gate Bridge and hike to the top of the Marin Headlands just to take in its breathtaking sights. We walked around the different neighborhoods and the waterfront. We got to know each other well. I was sure he knew I was gay.

Jim turned me on to LSD one weekend, and we went for a long hike around the Presidio, where we were stationed. I took off my shoes and walked barefoot through the pine needles on the forest floor, drunk on the rushing thoughts and images swirling in my brain. Exhilarated beyond rapture, I ended up flat on my back, looking up through the tall trees to the sun, feeling the earth move under me, tasting tears of unbridled joy that streamed down my face into my mouth. I felt perfect, loved by God.

Later, when the drug started wearing off and I could speak a coherent sentence, Jim led me back to the barracks, where we undressed and took a long, hot shower together. He washed my back and looked deeply into my dilated eyes. His touch turned me on, but I was afraid we'd be found out, so nothing happened. Instead we smoked pot and listened to Led Zeppelin and the Who's rock opera *Tommy*. All the while, I fell deeper and deeper into the sparkling pools of love in his eyes.

A few weeks later, we took acid again. This time, we ended up off base at a party in the Dolores Street Victorian flat of one of the army nursing school instructors. After midnight, when most everyone had left, we lay down on a big bed, where other guys from the base had passed out. Jim pulled my head to rest on his shoulder. He held my hand in his, stroked every finger gently, and then sucked on them. I had a raging hard-on and I hoped this would be it.

I led him into the dining room and we stopped under the chandelier in the burgundy velvet darkness. Jim pulled me close, grasping my throbbing crotch, and whispered, "I love you." Nobody had ever said that to me before. Then he kissed me, his tongue on mine, deeply and for a long time. We fell to the plush pile carpet in a loving embrace and he unzipped my pants and took my dick in his mouth. I was not really sure about the finer points of giving my first blow job, but I fumbled awkwardly in an effort to reciprocate. In a sixty-nine position, we both shot sperm at the same time. Afterward, we found a room with an empty bed and fell asleep in each other's arms for a couple of hours. We woke up and did it again, this time taking off all our clothes. I'd had some sex before, but I knew I was making love for the first time.

The next day, I was in full afterglow. But Jim got nervous, afraid we'd be exposed and punished. After that evening, we only occasionally got it on, as there was no privacy in our lives. But we stayed close friends. At the end of the nursing program, we were assigned to different hospitals. He went off to Okinawa, and I had the luck to be remain stationed in San Francisco.

I dreamed about him every night. A while later, I heard from a friend that Jim had gotten married and gone back to Tennessee. I cried, but I wasn't going to go back into the closet and get married like him. I was not going to lie about being gay anymore. Falling in love with Jim had changed me. The power of love opened my closet door.

I told my parents I was gay at Christmas. They said I was going to hell and we did not speak again for ten years.

I finished up my enlistment and was honorably discharged from the army in February 1972. I decided to stay in San Francisco and get involved in gay rights.

San Francisco is a sweet addiction, a spell cast deep into the blood. Junkie romantics get high on a feeling of being at the center of the universe, fixating on the city's most precious natural resource: freedom. San Francisco is a city made for lovers. It is providence that homosexuals have lived openly behind its golden gates for more than a century. Lavender tolerance and social acceptance are fabled there as much as its Victorian architecture.

I didn't come to sewing easily—even though sewing was etched into the genes of both my grandmother and my mother. Grandma ran a men's clothing shop and knew all the tricks of fine tailoring. My mother made matching outfits for herself and my two younger sisters. But she was unlikely to teach me a woman's skill.

However, I took up the family tradition in 1972 when my friend Mary Dunn got out her Singer sewing machine and sat me down for my first lesson. Mary was an earth mother, and she wanted to nurture my lust for beautiful clothing, which she shared. We'd met while doing campaign work for presidential candidate George McGovern and for Proposition 19 on the California ballot, which attempted to legalize marijuana in the state. Mary and I would get together after my science classes at San Francisco State University, smoke a couple of joints, and then read through the latest copies of *Vogue* and knock off the designers we liked. We followed every tidbit of gossip about Halston and Yves Saint-Laurent and imagined living in New York and Paris.

I started showing up to math class wearing my latest creations. Glam rock stars were coming on the scene then, and it seemed normal to dress like David Bowie in satin pants and a ruffled shirt. I bought a pair of platform shoes, and I grew my hair and styled it in the shoulder-length pageboy made immortal by Barbra Streisand.

My sewing was crude. I would skip things like buttons and pockets because they took too much time. I was in a hurry to wear whatever ensemble was on the cutting table. Mary complained about this, having been taught to stitch the old-fashioned way, using patterns in her high school home economics class. She would make every little stitch by hand first. And she didn't skip buttons and zippers. Mary wondered how I could wear pants without pockets. My solution? I carried a purse.

Mary was firm that I should get serious and start making pockets and buttonholes. She said it would be good for me to get some real sewing tutoring, since we were running out of ideas to extrapolate from the McCall's and Butterick pattern catalogs.

I enrolled in a summer tailoring course at San Francisco City College. I was the only man in a class of women. The instructor first had everyone bring in something they had made. I showed off gold metallic satin trousers I had created for a Grateful Dead concert. The teacher displayed them to the class, holding them up as if they might be full of lice. She pointed out the extremely poor construction and explained that this was an example of what not to do. Instead, we would all make gray flannel blazers.

Singer Camille O'Grady works it out with David in the new lame jeans by Gilbert. Be sure to avoid retinal damage under disco lights when wearing these flashy, reflective pants. Radar jeans are definitely beyond vision.

An early creation: "Radar jeans" sewn by emerging designer "Gilbert." *Photo and ad by Mark Rennie*

I pinned. I cut. I basted. I ironed. But I knew I would never wear anything as boring as gray flannel. At one point, I asked the teacher when we would get to create from our own designs. I proposed making a pink jumpsuit. The class laughed. The instructor just glared at me.

Mary told me that sewing wasn't always about being creative. Home economics classes were designed to teach women how to be housewives. Knowing how to make one's own clothes was a way to save the breadwinner money. Every woman would need a gray flannel blazer. But I started wondering why only women were taught sewing. Men should really be the ones to make the clothing; after all, they are builders, engineers. The process of cutting fabric and hammering it through powerful machines to become armor against the elements seemed masculine, even warrior-like.

I didn't need a gray flannel blazer. I didn't like the teacher. I didn't like the students. I didn't like the way I felt like a eunuch in a harem of Stepford Wives. I dropped out of class after two weeks and started paying attention to the women's liberation movement instead.

Great bonfires of burning bras were suddenly on the front page. Having been out as a homosexual for less than two years, I was beginning to understand that gay men were going to play a pivotal role in the redefinition of gender and power. The women's movement was intrinsically connected to our struggle because we were up against the same thing: an army of gray flannel suits.

To celebrate my escape from a summer of academic torture, I made myself a getup from tapestry to wear to a Rolling Stones concert at the Winterland Ballroom. It was skintight with a cape and without pockets. Mary and I sat in a haze of hashish, mesmerized by Their Satanic Majesties. I suddenly noticed that Mick Jagger had little pockets on his velvet pants. A few days later, I called my grandmother in Kansas and asked how to improve my sewing skills. She told me to practice.

So I practiced sewing for five years. By 1977, I was confident enough in my work that I began to make things for other people, like Halloween costumes and gowns for drag queens. I also began making protest banners for the almost-daily demonstrations organized by the left in San Francisco.

I had moved to the Fillmore neighborhood by then, but my spiritual and political home was a few blocks away at 330 Grove Street. This was the big, old, three-story brick building recently named the Gay Community Center. The grandeur of its Beaux-Arts granite pediments and limestone colonnades stood in contrast to its dilapidated neighborhood, full of old brick factories and wooden sheds. The Center was run by the Pride Foundation. The foundation had gotten a lease from a city housing agency that had jurisdiction over the building. Every morning, I'd walk down the hill to this nerve center of the gay revolution. It was where I would eventually create the Rainbow Flag.

The first floor had tall ceilings and a big open bay, surrounded by a sagging mezzanine. Under bare lightbulbs and exposed wooden beams, crowds would gather regularly for meetings and to organize actions. One of the first was the creation of the Coalition for Human Rights, formed in 1977 out of necessity to create an organization for everyone to unite against government oppression and other social challenges. People were furious about anti-gay discrimination and violence against our community. Hundreds came to the meetings and thousands showed up for our protest marches.

The coalition included several committees for people to plug into: outreach, media, actions, elections, etc. One of them was the graphics committee. This was my place to dive in. Our meetings had no round-robin ideological debates, no Robert's Rules of Order. Our job was to make the visuals: flyers, posters, T-shirts, placards, banners. Everything needed to declare our messages. Our only agenda was just to get it done and make it fabulous. It was all about art as a political tool.

Tandy Belew introduced himself at one of the coalition meetings. He was a miniature Zeus, a bearded blond god in Levi's 501s and a tight Lacoste shirt. My heart stopped; it was love at first sight. He liked me right off the bat, and when the big meeting broke up into workshops, we both headed over to the corner where the graphics committee was gathering.

A commercial graphic artist, Tandy had tremendous talent. We became the cochairs of the graphics group, and in short order he was teaching me Letraset—the sheets of adhesive letters in different typefaces that we used to create printed materials.

To raise money for the committee, we decided to make T-shirts and sell them for five dollars. Tandy got access to a silk-screen studio on Fourteenth Street one afternoon and showed me how to use it. The ink used in the process makes you very high. Tandy played music by Keith Jarrett to keep things mellow. By day's end, we had 288 white cotton T-shirts printed and hung to dry.

Tandy had the soul of a true artist. Just being around him made me feel like one. He was generous with his knowledge and patient with his instruction. I soaked up everything. Thus began my long fascination with a new craft.

The silk-screened T-shirts sold out immediately, and the graphics committee got a couple hundred dollars to use for the upcoming 1977 Gay Freedom Day.

On our rounds, we were a very dynamic gay duo. Tandy would look sharp and clean-cut, while I'd look fabulous in high heels and flowing hair. I had a very androgynous glamour, passing as a woman without the drag of trying to look like one. Once, I got a meeting with the president of City College. I got him to let us use John Adams Community College in the Haight for a workshop, negotiating the whole deal while wearing thirteen-button navy bellbottoms, a white beaded sweater, jangling bracelets, gold lamé platforms, and a Jean Shrimpton shag hairdo. Tandy was amazed.

Hundreds of people pitched in that year to make us all kinds of props and signs for the march. Arts and crafts were a fun way for everyone to get involved—even those not politically minded. On the

Amid rising outrage over anti-gay discrimination, Gilbert and the graphics committee created a provocative tableau at the 1977 Gay Freedom Day Parade.
Marie Ueda Collection (2006-12), courtesy of the Gay, Lesbian, Bisexual, Transgender Historical Society

day of the 1977 parade, more than 250,000 people showed up, carrying a sea of signs and banners. It was the largest gay event ever.

Soon after the parade, I took an apartment right above Tandy's on Collingwood Street in the heart of the Castro district. I put up royal blue satin on the living room walls. Summer turned to autumn and Tandy and my attraction heated up, despite us being exact opposites. He was butch and I was femme. Short hair versus long hair, muscular versus skinny.

The idea of a sex change had first crossed my mind in childhood. It was more than just wearing dresses, which felt natural; there were also my notions about gender. I questioned my own stereotypes: the ways I divided things between pink and blue, between feminine and masculine. I wondered if I was a woman trapped in a man's body.

Ultimately, I didn't surgically remove my penis. But I didn't stop wearing dresses. I never used a drag name. I was always Gilbert.

5

Stitching a Rainbow

Harvey Milk was the leading light and lightning rod for the gay community in San Francisco. I'd known him since 1975. When I met him, I instantly felt a sense of connection with his daring and hope. But not everybody liked him; old-timers who ran the local bar scene didn't welcome this hippie newcomer from New York. Yet Harvey's aura was irresistible—he was someone taking power, not waiting for it to be given. "Come out" was Harvey's mantra. He called on homosexuals everywhere to leave the prison of the closet for the freedom of the truth. He was a passionate and riveting speaker. When he said something, his words lifted and inspired people like Moses.

For gay men and lesbians, coming out is a moment of emancipation from which there is no turning back. Coming out in 1971 was the most important moment in my life. I was now proud to be a foot soldier in Harvey's army. We were all on a journey to the promised land. Light beckoned.

That expanding circle of supporters got Harvey Milk elected to office in November 1977. He was the first openly gay person to take the constitutional oath in the grand oak chambers of the San Francisco Board of Supervisors. He had an office and a new staff in city hall—a seat at the table of power.

The Center at 330 Grove Street was just a block from the great bronze-domed seat of city government. But ideologically they were miles apart. Harvey soon found himself at odds with those from the Center and its grassroots politics. His practice of radical, in-your-face inclusion did not sit well with some. And when Harvey went to city hall, the Gay Community Center was suddenly eclipsed as the center of the gay universe.

There was also a storm brewing over the name of the group that ran the annual parade in June. They were known first as the Gay Freedom Day Committee. But people were lobbying for the word *lesbian* to be added to the title. It set the stage for a conflict. Meetings were held and debates fired up. If we accept a name change, people wondered, does the word *lesbian* go before or after the word *gay* in the group's name? People took sides. There were screaming matches.

Divides opened about gender and identity, and they split even further along generational lines. Paul Hardman ran the Pride Foundation and Celeste Newbrough ran the parade committee. Their styles clashed loudly—blue-blooded, monied old-boy network versus radical Berkeley dykes. Paul, a rotund Pacific Heights gay businessman, wore a suit and tie every day. Celeste never varied from a plaid flannel shirt and flak vest over blue jeans and Birkenstocks. They hated each other.

Harvey Milk was smart enough to stay a step removed from the turf war over the organization of the parade. Harvey was the commanding general, focused on the big picture. But he was also savvy enough to put one of his staffers right in the middle of it. Milk protégé Cleve Jones soon took over the parade committee's media coordination.

I'd known Cleve since he moved to the city as a fresh-faced, curly-haired film student from Arizona. I watched him become part of Harvey's trusted inner circle. Cleve was Harvey's lieutenant in charge of organizing the huge street protests, which were almost daily events. We were both twenty years younger than everyone around us, and we became friends.

We hung out at Café Flore, went for walks though the hilltop forests, and dished the dirt while doing the dishes after potluck dinners. We were always exchanging political ideas. I would often get a midnight call from him, saying we'd be having an action in the morning and asking me to make a banner. So I'd get out of bed and Cleve would come over. We'd shove the gowns aside, dig through my rag pile, cut out letters, and then I'd stitch up a GAY RIGHTS NOW banner while Cleve worked the phone to spread the word.

The work was fun. Cleve's sense of humor and outrageous courage turned me on. He was smart, with frequent flashes of genius. He was cute for sure; all the old guys at the Pride Foundation had a hard-on for him. Cleve knew it and flirted shamelessly.

But I wasn't in love with Cleve; I was still in love with Tandy Belew.

Tandy had broken my heart. Our affair ended suddenly over the Christmas holidays in complete disillusionment. I wrote a sad, indulgent epic poem of unrequited passion.

To get over him, I devoted myself further to activism and went to the movies. My friend Artie Bressan Jr. was a filmmaker who had just made a documentary about the 1977 parade, titled *Gay USA*. He was a wild visionary who directed porn on the side to finance his 35 mm documentaries. We went to see films several times a week.

One day, we went to the Strand Theater on Market Street to see *Citizen Kane*. It was Artie's favorite. Cleve joined us. After the movie, we all walked over to Civic Center Plaza to look at the neoclassic buildings. Artie began to press me to come up with a new symbol for what he had called "the dawn of a new gay consciousness and freedom." Both he and Harvey had brought this idea up to me before.

At this point, the pink triangle was the symbol for the gay movement. But it represented a dark chapter in the history of same-sex rights. The pink triangle was used by the Germans to mark homosexuals during World War II in the same way the Star of David was used against Jews. It functioned as a Nazi tool of oppression. We all felt that we needed something that was positive, that celebrated our love.

As Artie implored, I looked at the flags flying on the various government buildings around the Civic Center. I thought of the original American flag with its thirteen stripes and thirteen stars, the colonies breaking away from England to form the United States. I thought of the vertical red, white, and blue tricolor from the French Revolution, and how both flags owed their beginnings to a riot, a rebellion, or a revolution. I thought a gay nation should have a flag too, to proclaim its own idea of power.

As a community, both local and international, gay people were in the midst of an upheaval, a battle for equal rights, a shift in status in which we were now demanding power—and taking it. This was our new revolution: a tribal, individualistic, and collective vision. It deserved a new symbol.

Earlier in my adult life, when I thought of a flag, I saw it as just another icon to lampoon. I had come to consider all flag-waving and patriotism in general to be a dangerous joke. But that changed in 1976. The celebration of the US bicentennial put the focus on the American flag. It was everywhere, from pop art to fine art, from tacky souvenirs to trashy advertising. On every level, it functioned as a message. After the orgy of bunting and hoopla surrounding the bicentennial, I thought of flags in a new light. I discovered the depth of their power, their transcendent, transformational quality. I thought of the emotional connection they hold. I thought how most flags represented a place. They were primarily nationalistic, territorial, iconic propaganda—all things we questioned in the '70s. Gay people were both tribal and individualistic, a global collective that was expressing itself in art and politics. We needed a flag to fly everywhere.

My imagination was stirred. Cleve and I parted from Artie and went dancing. The Winterland Ballroom at Steiner and Post was our favorite playground. I loved the discos and the Stud Bar, but we went to Winterland to hear live rock 'n' roll music in the broken-down plaster palace. The former ice show arena had been transformed by impresario Bill Graham into a larger version of his legendary Fillmore Auditorium. Upstairs was a big balcony that seated several thousand, who were free to make out and smoke pot. The main floor, where snow queens once ice skated, was a smooth cement dance floor.

Cleve and I danced the same way: we always raised our arms up over our heads, snapping our fingers like Diana Ross. We'd shake our hips like Tina Turner, acid cheerleaders twirling in psychedelic, funkadelic circles.

The crowd was as much a part of the show as the band. Everyone was there: North Beach beatniks and barrio zoots, the bored bikers in black leather, teenagers in the back row kissing. There were long-haired, lithe girls in belly-dance getups, pink-haired punks safety-pinned together, hippie suburbanites, movie stars so beautiful they left you dumbstruck, muscle gayboys with perfect mustaches, butch dykes in blue jeans, and fairies of all genders in thrift-store dresses. We rode the mirrored ball on glittering LSD and love power. Dance fused us, magical and cleansing. We were all in a swirl of color and light. It was like a rainbow.

A rainbow. That's the moment when I knew exactly what kind of flag I would make.

A Rainbow Flag was a conscious choice, natural and necessary. The rainbow came from earliest recorded history as a symbol of hope. In the book of Genesis, it appeared as proof of a covenant between God and all living creatures. It was also found in Chinese, Egyptian, and Native American history. A Rainbow Flag would be our modern alternative to the pink triangle. Now the rioters who had claimed their freedom at the Stonewall Inn in 1969 would have their own symbol of liberation.

For years, San Francisco's Gay Freedom Day Parade had been the responsibility of gay bar and business owners. But as it evolved, it attracted participation from the broader community. By 1977, the parade—some called it a march—had grown to hundreds of thousands. In 1978, Harvey Milk got the city to support it for the first time. Ten thousand dollars went to the Pride Foundation, its nonprofit sponsor.

It was June 14, 1978—Flag Day. I was at the Gay Community Center at the tiny cubicle office on the mezzanine that served as march headquarters. Cleve was already at the folding table by the window that he used as his media committee desk.

"You want a thousand dollars to make flags?" Celeste Newbrough asked, looking me right in the eye. The expenditure had already been approved by the parade committee, but clearly Celeste wanted to remind me who was boss, and to reassert her group's authority over how I planned to spend their money.

GAY FREEDOM DAY 1978

GAY FREEDOM DAY COMMITTEE Pride Foundation

May 10, 1978

Dear Mr. Bloomfield:

I am writing to you at the suggestion of Bonnie Hughes at the Museum of Art. This year's Gay Freedom Day Parade & Celebration will be June 25th, and as a part of those festivites a committee to decorate Civic Center Plaza has been formed. We're focusing our effort on a restoration of the decoration of City Hall which was completed for the Panama Pacific Exhibition of 1915. We plan to employ the use of garlands and various buntings to hang on the Polk Street facade. The Neighborhood Arts Program is assisting us with volunteers and some materials, the Eureka/Noe Valley Artists Coalition is providing us with space at the Top Floor Gallery, 300 Grove Street. We're planning this event as a Community Art Project and will be encouraging the participation of everyone in the Bay area through the radio, television, and newspaper coverage of this event.

Ms. Hughes suggested to me that you might be able to help in our research of the documents describing and illustrating the decoration of City Hall in the past. We understand that you have extensive information about the Civic Center in your files on the Opera House.

I would like to make arrangements to see any data or hear any information you might think would be helpful to us in our effort. The Committee to Decorate Civic Center Plaza meets every Tuesday night at 7:30. I'm hopeful you might come to one of our meetings. In June we will be working every day with a large number of volunteer artists in our cooperative creative construction of the decorations.

Sincerely yours,

Gilbert Baker
Chair, Decoration Committee

Mailing Address: 1 United Nations Plaza, San Francisco, CA 94102
Office: 330 Grove Street   Telephone: (415) 863-9893

COMPLIMENTS OF Job Jobs Printing Company   932 Howard Street   San Francisco, Ca 94103 Telephone: 777-4567

Letter from Gilbert, chairman of the 1978 decoration committee, requesting specs for Civic Center Plaza. *Courtesy of the ONE Archives at the USC Libraries*

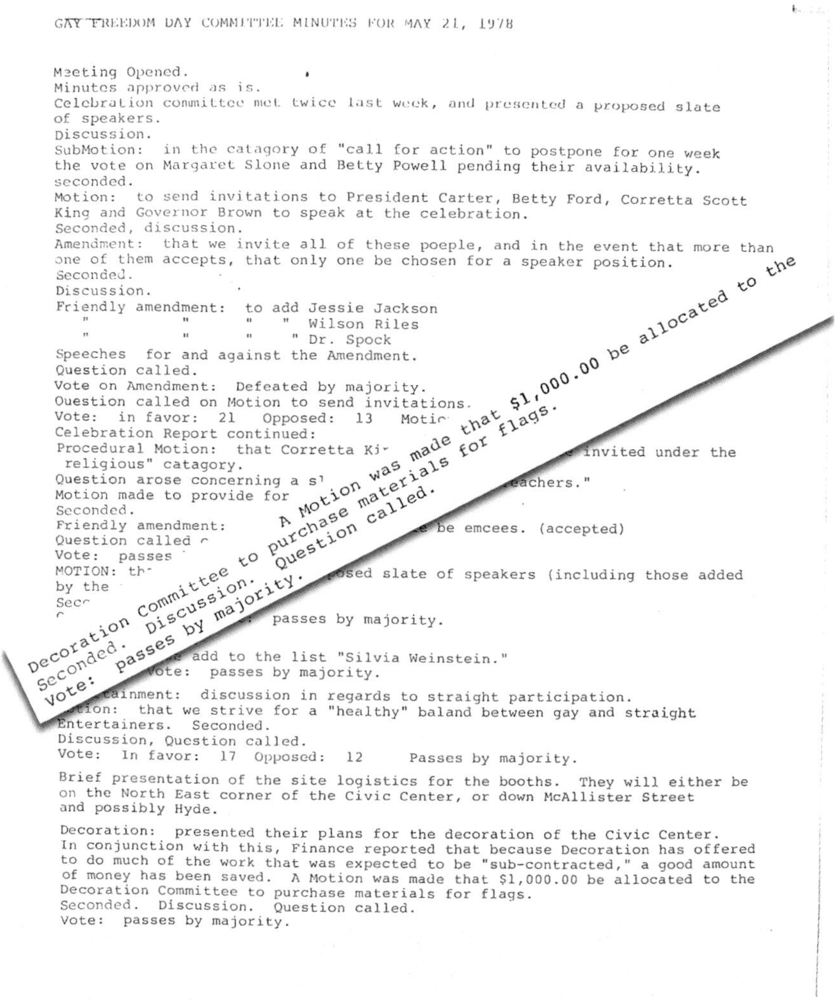

Meeting Opened.
Minutes approved as is.
Celebration committee met twice last week, and presented a proposed slate
of speakers.
Discussion.
SubMotion: in the catagory of "call for action" to postpone for one week
the vote on Margaret Slone and Betty Powell pending their availability.
seconded.
Motion: to send invitations to President Carter, Betty Ford, Corretta Scott
King and Governor Brown to speak at the celebration.
Seconded, discussion.
Amendment: that we invite all of these poeple, and in the event that more than
one of them accepts, that only one be chosen for a speaker position.
Seconded.
Discussion.
Friendly amendment: to add Jessie Jackson
      "   "   "   " Wilson Riles
      "   "   "   " Dr. Spock
Speeches for and against the Amendment.
Question called.
Vote on Amendment: Defeated by majority.
Question called on Motion to send invitations.
Vote: in favor: 21   Opposed: 13   Motio*_____ *invited under the
Celebration Report continued:
Procedural Motion: that Corretta K*_____ *achers."
  religious" catagory.
Question arose concerning a s*_____
Motion made to provide for _____ be emcees. (accepted)
Seconded.
Friendly amendment: _____
Question called *_____ *osed slate of speakers (including those added
Vote: passes *
MOTION: th*_____
by the *_____ passes by majority.
Sec*
*_____ add to the list "Silvia Weinstein."
*_____ *ote: passes by majority.
*_____ainment: discussion in regards to straight participation.
*_ion: that we strive for a "healthy" baland between gay and straight
Entertainers. Seconded.
Discussion, Question called.
Vote: In favor: 17 Opposed: 12   Passes by majority.

Brief presentation of the site logistics for the booths. They will either be
on the North East corner of the Civic Center, or down McAllister Street
and possibly Hyde.

Decoration: presented their plans for the decoration of the Civic Center.
In conjunction with this, Finance reported that because Decoration has offered
to do much of the work that was expected to be "sub-contracted," a good amount
of money has been saved. A Motion was made that $1,000.00 be allocated to the
Decoration Committee to purchase materials for flags.
Seconded. Discussion. Question called.
Vote: passes by majority.

[Rotated overlaid text:]

A Motion was made that $1,000.00 be allocated to the
Decoration Committee to purchase materials for flags.
Seconded. Discussion. Question called.
Vote: passes by majority.

Minutes from the parade committee authorizing the $1,000 for the creation
of Rainbow Flags. *Courtesy of the ONE Archives at the USC Libraries*

She wrinkled her brow and looked me over. My hair was past my shoulders and I was wearing a dress. She was in her midforties with a short Dorothy Hamill hairdo, and decked out in her standard baggy blue jeans and red flannel lumberjack shirt. I chuckled at our fashion role reversal.

Just then, Paul Hardman was coming down the hallway. He stopped dead in his tracks before our door and eavesdropped.

I took a deep breath and explained, "Five hundred dollars for a thousand yards of muslin, fifty-eight inches wide. Three hundred dollars for ten pounds of natural dye in eight colors, and a hundred pounds of salt and ash. And the rest for art supplies."

"Show them the picture," Cleve said, backing me up as we had planned.

I dropped my sketch on Cleve's desk and added simply, "Rainbow Flags at United Nations Plaza. I need a thousand dollars."

Hardman came in. He looked at the drawing, gave Celeste the evil eye, smiled at Cleve, and gave me a curt nod of approval before returning to the hallway to linger.

But Celeste was not sold. I explained my plan to make the flags here at the Center, up on the top floor in back of the art gallery.

"A thousand dollars, eight colors. *Hmm.*" Celeste calculated the costs, adding, "Flags? I don't like flags."

Cleve intervened. "Tell her about the colors, what they mean."

I took a deep breath and explained loudly so everyone, including Paul, could hear. "Pink is for sex. Red is for life. Orange is for healing. Yellow is for the sun. Green is for nature. Turquoise is for magic. Blue is for serenity. Purple is for the spirit. Every color has a meaning just like the American flag—symbolism all the way," I said.

"You're just making that up," Celeste laughed.

Paul Hardman, still out in the hallway, chimed in loudly, "I read that in the *Kama Sutra* or somewhere."

Celeste looked at me, paused, and finally said "OK." Suddenly, she took a blank check from the breast pocket of her shirt and signed it. As she did, Hardman poked his head in again. Celeste made sure he saw her handing the check to me.

"Cleve," she ordered, "put it in the decoration committee budget. And don't fuck it up, Gilbert." She paused. "I'll have to call you Betsy Ross," she laughed.

I skipped away with the check and my new project. Betsy Ross? That's funny, I thought. Nobody has ever called me that before.

I got a ride over to Haight-Ashbury, paid Linda at Discount Fabrics for the material, and loaded up the station wagon with bales of raw Chinese muslin. Walking west a block into my favorite art supply store, Mendel's, I found the owner, Bette, at the checkout counter. She was waiting with a big box of dyes, salt, ash, and special detergents. On the way back to the Gay Community Center, I picked up my Kenmore sewing machine.

By four in the afternoon, I had it all upstairs in the top-floor gallery at 330 Grove Street. The elements of the Rainbow Flag were ready to go. Cleve had bought me a desk phone for my new flag workshop. I needed help and there wasn't much time. I called up two talented friends, James McNamara and Faerie Argyle, who both loved fashion and fabric. James knew how to sew pretty well; he had gone a semester or two at the Fashion Institute of Technology in New York City. Faerie was the queen of tie-dye and a part of the Angels of Light theatrical troupe, a spin-off from the Cockettes. We all knew each other from the rock shows at Winterland, where we ruled the dance floor with Cleve.

James and Faerie soon showed up. Pushing our way through the debris that had piled up in the back of the gallery, we found a place where there weren't any holes in the roof. The three of us cleaned up with brooms and dustpans, clearing a place to set up the workshop.

As we unpacked the bales of muslin, Faerie and I noticed it had a slightly starched feel; there was some kind of sizing on the fiber. She informed me that it had to be in a raw natural state before the dying process, so we would first have to wash and dry all of the material to remove the sizing. As we unrolled the muslin, there was so much material that we decided to cut the bolts into manageable pieces. Then we headed to the closest big laundromat, located in the Castro.

Once there, we filled every one of the twenty-four washing machines and poured in gallons of organic detergent that we got at a health food store. We set the buttons on hot and went for wheatgrass juice. We returned in a while to watch the spin cycle. Then we put the material into dryers, still quite damp. We had forgotten to budget for this step of the process. We spent more than twenty dollars in quarters drying the endless loads.

When we opened up the dryers, the fabric was twisted into a thousand knots. After we dropped the fabric back at the workshop, Faerie and I went home for irons. The ironing would take days. We would burn up Sunbeam irons and blow fuses hourly at the Center. It was getting dark when we finally dumped the last of more than four hundred pounds of cloud-white cotton on the top floor. It was a big heap that looked like many futons jumbled together. We jumped into it. It felt divine.

The next morning, we got under way. Brand-new, jumbo black garbage cans were filled with water. We had sixteen of the fifty-gallon plastic containers, two for each color. In old coffee cans, we began mixing the powdered dyes according to the instructions. We were using natural dyes at Faerie's insistence; they were very saturated and all seemed to be the same murky shade. As if we were scientists, we carefully stirred until the pigments were properly dissolved, then poured the colors into the sixteen receptacles.

Slowly, we pushed the first piece of white cloth into a garbage can marked RED. Red is the hardest color to dye, and usually more expensive, so we wanted to make sure it would work. We dipped in a few yards for a moment, and then lifted it out. It was gorgeous. It took an hour to fill the two red dye baths with a hundred yards of fabric, cut into varying lengths. The dye job had to be very even, requiring us to move the fabric all around as it soaked up the pigment.

We noticed our hands and arms were getting stained. When we finished and went to wash up, we had a surprise. The red dye didn't come off with organic soap. It didn't come off with Lava soap. Neither

Comet nor bleach worked. It didn't come off at all. Our arms and hands were stained for weeks. We looked like ax murderers.

For a full week, the cloth incubated in the pigment soup. Every day, we would swish the fabric around. When it was time, we poured out the dye and refilled each barrel with fresh water, adding ash to set the salt dye and make it permanent.

A few days later, the dyed muslin was ready to come out. We had to rinse it, but it was so heavy with water that we couldn't move it. Upstairs on the roof of 330 Grove was an old fire hydrant. Faerie and I took some of the fabric up there to see if maybe we could wash out the residue. When we turned on the water, it shot out across the top of the building and ran down a brick wall. Piece by piece, we brought the flag fabric over to the jet of water so that the shooting gusher would splash through it. Color ran everywhere, soaking us. We took off all our clothes to continue the work.

One of the members of Dykes on Bikes, Glenne McElhinney, came up to see what we were doing. She had seen the dye dripping down the building. She took off her clothes and joined the operation. The three of us methodically rinsed out each section of dyed goods and put them back into empty garbage cans. Glenne, I noticed, was checking out Faerie.

Our rinsing wasn't working; there was still too much pigment left, and it stained anything that it touched. The only answer seemed to be washing it again with detergent. We loaded the fabric into plastic bags and, after much effort, got it downstairs and into a car.

They always have signs in laundries saying, No DYEING ALLOWED. We figured we better go to a neighborhood where nobody knew us. We found an empty laundry on Gough Street. As the washers spun with our items, we waited in the car across the street as if we were criminals. After the spin cycle, we quickly stuffed the muslin into fresh bags. Before we made our getaway, we left each machine running with a cup of bleach, hoping the next customers wouldn't be surprised by pink underwear.

Back at the workshop, we began ironing the entire one thousand yards for the second time. The fabric was alive, it was so vibrant. Faerie had been right: there is simply no comparison to natural dye. I had never seen color so intense, and I had taken many trips on LSD. It was so soft and sumptuous to the touch, we couldn't take our hands off it. We lovingly caressed each bit of it as we steamed out every crease.

On a folding table from a school cafeteria, I set up my little Kenmore sewing machine. I started winding up the bobbins. This was going to take a lot of thread. I tinkered with the tension, adjusting it so that each stitch would be perfect. We cut some little test samples and I sewed them up so we could determine how to proceed. The flags would have to be very strong to hold up in the gales that blew through San Francisco. I picked through the many long bolt pieces and selected one of each color, making certain each length was evenly dyed and at least sixty feet long.

James was now back to help. Together we managed to haul my larger industrial Singer sewing machine up to the top floor to speed our mammoth task. My hands worked the #14 needle into place. Each time I stepped on the foot presser, the Singer machine whirred for a few seconds and two more inches of thread locked the fabric in place.

During the many hours of work, James, Faerie, and I discussed what we were doing and what it would mean to the community and to the movement. We knew that flags were political statements. As artists, we hoped that the Rainbow Flag might be the antithesis of all flags, its meaning more about nature, which united us, than nationalities, which divided us. To reject the notion of a protocol over which stripe had to be on top or bottom when the banner was on display, we made two Rainbow Flags. We'd hang one with the pink stripe on the top and the other with the pink stripe on the bottom. "We are a versatile people," James joked in reference to talk of tops and bottoms, all New Jersey accent and Fashion Institute of Technology bitchiness.

Meanwhile, Faerie was block-dyeing her own idea for a flag. She was cutting a special piece of blue for a field of stars in a circle, which she would patch into one of the two Rainbow Flags. "If you ask me," Faerie said, "flags are boring, but sex is interesting. Fucking is the real revolution. Putting the two together, you'll be the Gay Betsy Ross,"

Faerie said and giggled. "I can see you now, gray hair and spectacles, rocking in a chair, telling someone else's grandchildren about how it was, screwing our brains out and sewing."

Faerie suddenly had an idea. "We should take our clothes off and roll around in the flag before we fly it. You know, give it a naked and raw energy. A flag about gay sex ought to be covered in it." I felt the sparkle of excitement. We stripped and our naked flesh sprawled across the soft contours of the two cotton banners, fresh from the sewing machines.

———————

It was the morning of June 25, 1978. I hadn't slept the night before. I finished the final stitches of the two huge flags, each one thirty by sixty feet, just as the dawn broke and sunlight streamed into the workshop on the top floor of the Gay Community Center. Faerie had made everyone a breakfast of echinacea and ginseng tea and James had brought some cocaine that we were going to snort after we completed the sewing.

Around eight o'clock, I walked the few short blocks to United Nations Plaza, wanting to make certain we raised the enormous flags on the two poles before the wind came up. I wasn't totally certain they would hold together if a gale really started blowing. The forecast was for gusts up to forty miles per hour.

The flags were too large for the internal rigging mechanism on the poles, which usually held twenty-by-twenty-foot American and United Nations flags, one on each pole. So I improvised, adding a homemade rope collar at the bottom of the flag.

I'd made a test run a few days before, only to discover that the flag's heading, which holds it to the pole, was not strong enough. That flag had ripped in the full force of the wind. So I reconstructed the heading with a jute reinforcement and took it down to Paramount Flag Company. They stamped in large industrial brass grommets every foot so the flag could lace along the steel cable it would fly from. The wind was not up yet. I didn't chance it—I was planning to keep the flags furled until they were ready.

A gay attorney named Walter Caplan owned a small wedge of a building that faced directly onto United Nations Plaza. He was Harvey Milk's lawyer and had some other city connections, and I had asked him to help me get access to the flagpoles. The ropes were on the inside of the pole so vandals wouldn't be able to cut them. Walter was waiting for us when I arrived with Cleve and a few friends. He held a little crank handle in his hands, mysteriously delivered to him by the Parks and Recreation Department.

Each flag was raised by means of a small windup spool that was behind a small locked door set into the base of the flagpole. Walter cranked the tiny ratchet as everyone held the first flag close to the pole. It was starting to blow open and you could see Faerie's field of tie-dyed stars, exploding overhead. Walter kept cranking. It went up higher and higher and got more impossible to hold onto. When the first breeze came up, it sailed out of our hands and rippled open.

Though fifty feet up the flagpole, the rainbow banner was still touching the ground, slashing back and forth across the brick pavement. We let it go so we could help Walter crank it up to the top. It took the combined strength of all of us; there was a blur of hands in a wild rowing motion as the flag began its ascent. The ratchet gizmo burned our hands.

The Rainbow Flag began snapping loudly in the wind. I never imagined a flag could make such a sound.

Within an hour, both flags were up and more than 250,000 people filled the sidewalks of Market Street in the Financial District, waiting for the start of the 1978 Gay Freedom Day Parade. It would be the largest ever; the multitude of humanity stretched as far as the eye could see. Another 100,000 people lined up in the assembly area south of the district. The police soon stopped trying to enforce order and traffic control.

Faerie, James, and I hurried back to the top floor of the Gay Community Center, where we changed out of our jeans and sweats and got dressed up for the big celebration. Everyone had put together something special to wear. We were out to show the world that we were fabulous, beautiful, and powerful. Faerie donned a silk tie-dyed kimono over layers of matching skirts and scarves. James was out to cruise, so he chose butt-tight white jeans and a white vest that showed off his gorgeous tan and muscular arms.

My dress was about twenty yards of white silk, all cut on the bias to blow wildly in the wind, inspired by the classical sculpture masterpiece Winged Victory. In a touch of sacrilege, I had created a large drape over one shoulder in blood-red velvet. The whole thing was complemented by a pair of clear Lucite high-heeled sandals. My hair was long and I had a beard. It was Glamour Jesus all the way.

Our friends met us at the Center and we passed around some joints while we arranged ourselves for display. Finally, our giggling entourage made its way down the old wooden staircase and out the front door toward United Nations Plaza. We wanted to check on the flags one last time to make sure they were not ripping in the monster wind blowing in from the Pacific Ocean.

When we got there, Walter Caplan came running up in a panic. In raising the banners, we had stripped the gears of the two flagpoles, he said; we would not be able to get them down again. The Rainbow Flags would simply fly until the wind shredded them. I loved the idea that we would never be able to touch the flags again, an offering to the Great Spirit. Walter had more news: damaging the flagpole gears meant we had ruined city property worth $90,000. We didn't care; those flagpoles belonged to the people. For the rest of the day, Walter went around calling me "the King."

People looked skyward to see the Rainbow Flags, their hands reaching up and their mouths open in astonishment. The winds blasted the banners so they strained against the cables. I expected them at any moment to blow away and go sailing up Market Street through a canyon of skyscrapers.

Our feet were dancing on air as we swirled our way up Market Street to where the parade was about to start. Church bells rang out at eleven o'clock as a roar of motorcycles erupted from the Dykes on Bikes contingent, scheduled to lead the parade to city hall. We were so stoned, we could feel the sound waves hitting us. There were hundreds of lesbian bikers, including Glenne McElhinney—wild women having a good time on the ultimate symbol of machine sexuality, the motorcycle. Some of them were topless. The butch factor had hit a new zenith, offset by a few Cinderellas and lipstick goddesses.

As we sashayed through the middle of them, the Dykes on Bikes whistled their appreciation for our sartorial splendor. Then they revved their engines into a crescendo and roared off. We just screamed our lungs out.

Suddenly, we were swept up in a tide of flesh. Celeste Newbrough and the parade committee came pushing up from behind. Cleve Jones and sex worker rights advocate Priscilla Alexander were both dressed in white, like suffragettes. They were carrying a large banner I'd created with Cleve that read, A SIMPLE MATTER OF JUSTICE. Behind them was a contingent of marching fists thrusting up to a chant of "The people united will never be defeated," loud enough that the windows vibrated on the buildings. Off in the distance, we could see City Supervisor Harvey Milk sitting on top of a convertible, draped with garlands and Hawaiian leis.

We opened up the piece of flag that had been cut away when we patched in Faerie's field of stars. As we carried it down the street, the crowd began tossing money at us and making wishes. A bizarre barrage of glittering coins flew all around us, some splashing onto the street. Drag queens approached and spread flowers in front of our footsteps. All these people understood what we had worked so hard to create and what it was all about. We laughed until we cried.

We made our way slowly through the throngs and got to United Nations Plaza, where we looked up to see the Rainbow Flags flicking and flying out over Market Street, like giant tongues of color licking the crowd. We listened to them crackle and pop. The Chinese muslin was thin enough to be slightly transparent in the sun. We had made a rainbow out of cloth.

Walter invited us into his offices, which looked out over the plaza and had a perfect view of the parade as it passed between the two enormous Rainbow Flags. We had mineral water and fruit and were laughing and making jokes. We competed in making terrible puns about flags and fags. Walter ushered in some city officials to meet us, including Supervisor Carol Ruth Silver, Supervisor Ella Hill Hutch, Supervisor so-and-so.

It soon became too much, so Faerie, James, and I retreated to the rooftop, where we could stretch out under the sun. We were at the closest point you could be physically to the flags, as though we could just reach out and touch them. We lay on the art deco rooftop and soaked in the energy of the parade, passing us only fifty feet below. Harvey Milk came riding up like the prophet crashing the gates. Waves of people crushed around him, at times lifting him into the air. He was our conquering hero, leading the masses toward city hall.

The crash of cymbals and the blare of trumpets announced a marching band. They played the old show tune "If My Friends Could See Me Now" and then "San Francisco" from the Jeanette MacDonald film of the same name. I could see drum major Jon Sims strutting and Tandy Belew puffing away on his tuba. They were giving it their all. We were hanging off the fire escape and cheering them on as they passed beneath the Rainbow Flags. We watched as hundreds of thousands filled up the many acres of San Francisco's Civic Center.

Around three o'clock, we joined Cleve as Harvey got up to speak on a flower-lined stage set up in front of city hall. He talked about a kid from Altoona who had called his office, desperate for support. Harvey reminded us how too many young people were trapped in desperate lives that ended in suicide. Harvey said we have to live our lives openly to inspire those suffering under oppression. "You've got to give them hope and hope and hope," he cried out. We believed him.

Cleve and I climbed on top of a big white truck and smoked a joint just as Sylvester took the stage. Sylvester was a big black drag queen who had a voice to rival Aretha Franklin. He had begun singing Bessie Smith and Billie Holiday blues songs as one of the Cockettes but then went disco. As he began singing his national hit, "You Make Me Feel (Mighty Real)," Cleve and I danced along.

"You know, this is really fucking great, Gilbert," Cleve said, suddenly getting serious.

"Yeah, well, it is pretty fabulous. All these people, Harvey, and everything."

"No, I mean what you've done is beautiful. It's history. A gay flag. Harvey's really proud of you."

"I'm proud of you, Cleve. It would never have happened without you and all the others." I hugged him and Cleve hugged back. "Brothers, then?"

"Brothers in arms!" Cleve shouted skyward toward the Rainbow Flags flying in the distance. He lit up another joint with great flourish and handed it to me, pledging, "Comrades! The people united will never be defeated."

When the sun went down, we all went home. The next morning, we were able to improvise a way to loosen the flagpole gears and lower the Rainbow Flags, but the poles would have to be restrung. We told Walter to send the bill for damages to the National Endowment for the Arts.

6

Victory and Backlash

Summer in San Francisco is foggy and cold. To escape, I went up to Sonoma Valley and spent the season with my friends Jill Gover and Tommy McConnell. They lived on a communal farm high above Bodega Bay. It was blazing hot; the thermometer outside Jill's little cabin read one hundred degrees. We spent our time doing the chores that come with primitive living. There was no running water, so we carried water. There was no electricity, so we chopped wood. We cooked over a wood stove and read books out loud in the evenings. It was paradise.

My city friends thought I was a very unlikely candidate for the rural lifestyle. Little did they know I had a closet full of evening gowns and high heels at the farm. Tommy, his boyfriend David Lee, Jill, her girlfriend Janis, and I would often dress up just for each other's amusement for dinner under the stars. Occasionally, we would drive over to the Russian River and go dancing in honky-tonk bars. More and more lesbians and gays were heading out of San Francisco and going north to find a quieter life. The sleepy little towns under the redwoods became a haven for lavender refugees getting away from urban decadence.

Every two weeks, we would descend on San Francisco in Tommy's old Ford truck for errands. We would pick up supplies and go scavenging for wood, windows, and doors. Tommy would use them in building his little house, which hung out over a steep canyon full of wild lilac.

Cleve would visit us at the ranch sometimes. He dreamed of one day building his own house somewhere in the country. He'd make little sketches all the time, which I loved for their ideas of symmetry and flow, and the way he wanted everything echoing nature. I always kept around a supply of different graph papers, vellums, and ruled tablets so we could draw together.

Cleve would ask me to take dictation when we worked together on something as simple as a cabin design. He was the fastest thinker around. We read each other's minds. I'd make notes and sketches for him. I wasn't Michelangelo, but I could get a reasonable idea on paper.

Meanwhile, Proposition 6 would be on the California ballot in November. Also known as the Briggs Initiative, after its author, conservative state legislator John Briggs, the measure would allow public schools to fire all lesbian and gay teachers. Pollsters were predicting that it was certain to pass, which would be a disastrous defeat for gay rights. Cleve was all over it and enlisted my help, calling me his art wizard—or art slave, depending on his mercurial moods. So I came back to San Francisco and we pitched in with all our might to help turn the vote around. He'd think nothing of calling me up at two o'clock in the morning with his latest brainstorm and asking me to pitch in.

Harvey Milk traveled around the state, speaking at rallies in high school gymnasiums. He debated right-wing bigots who supported Proposition 6, using his devastating humor on them, explaining that the public had more to fear from hate-mongers than homosexuals. I would attend these events and shout down the Prop 6 supporters. Soon, the good people of California started catching on that there was something intrinsically wrong and un-American about the campaign against us. Harvey had a word for it: *homophobia.*

I went to visit Walter Caplan, Harvey's lawyer, one Sunday afternoon. Harvey came over with his lieutenants, Dick Pabich and Jim Rivaldo. They were planning the final weeks of the closely contested election. They wanted some advice about color. Dick and Jim were about to print up thousands of signs and placards, at enormous cost, to support the "No on 6" counteroffensive. The materials would be posted statewide. They wanted to know what I thought about the color orange, what it signaled psychologically and spiritually. I remembered Faerie and James telling me that it represented healing, so I told them orange would be a good choice since Prop 6 was about hatred—a disease that needed healing. Besides, there was the very appealing idea of throwing the color orange into the faces of our enemies. Most Prop 6 supporters, including John Briggs, lived in Orange County.

On election night, I went down to Castro Street. Thousands had gathered there to wait for the results. Dick and Jim had rented out a nightclub around the corner for a victory party, and we hung the big Rainbow Flag behind the stage for a backdrop. Around eleven, Harvey stepped up to the microphone on the club stage and told us we had won. A spontaneous party exploded and poured out into the streets. It lasted for hours and culminated when cabaret singer Sharon McKnight stood on top of a newspaper kiosk at the corner of Castro and Eighteenth and belted out "The Battle Hymn of the Republic." Every voice filled the air with the chorus: *"Glory, glory hallelujah."* We had turned back the tide of recent electoral losses that had begun with Anita Bryant. We had stopped them with our ballots. We had done it in San Francisco. Now we had done it in California. Next, we would do it nationwide. Harvey called for a march on Washington, DC. Nothing would stop us.

With Prop 6 defeated, I returned to the farm. One day, Tommy picked up a guy named Morgan and brought him back to the ranch. Morgan was putting himself through college, writing film reviews for local gay newspapers. He was a big man—in every way, according to Tommy. Handsome, brilliant, and a great cook, Morgan often made wonderful dinners. Over them, we would dissect Hollywood films or the latest political developments. We became fast friends. I loved him like a brother.

We were making dinner a few days later when we heard on National Public Radio that something weird was going on in Jonestown. Jim Jones, a Bay Area radical preacher and self-styled guru, had moved his huge congregation of followers to Guyana, where they set up their own town. NPR reported that his cult had attracted a congressional investigation. We were very amused by this, since Jones had been a well-known political operative in San Francisco. On election days, he would turn his congregation, called the Peoples Temple, into a voting army. Everyone was fascinated when they went off to make their utopia in the jungle. California had become the cult capital of the world. It was a media story that was irresistible, right up there with Charlie Manson and Patty Hearst on the Richter scale of bizarre.

But a few days later, news came over our transistor radio that the cult members had all committed suicide. It seemed incredible. They had left behind a message: "Those who do not remember the past are condemned to repeat it." In the following days, as we prepared for Thanksgiving, more news about Jonestown emerged. All through our holiday feast, we listened to the latest gory reports. Morgan suggested we go down to San Francisco and watch it on television. He wanted to write an article about the Jonestown massacre, and I had an appointment in the city with Jon Beau Lee, a.k.a. Rainbow the Mime, who wanted some costumes made. His commissions kept me from starving. So we headed down. When we arrived, I bunked in with Faerie.

The next morning, November 27, Rainbow came over to pick me up at Faerie's tiny house. It was raining and we went driving around in his Volkswagen bus, shopping for fabric. He wanted a satin tuxedo made in the stripes of the rainbow. It was a Monday and we were hell-bent on our mission. We checked out our favorite stores in the Haight.

We were driving downtown with the radio on when suddenly we heard that Harvey Milk and Mayor George Moscone had been shot dead in city hall. I screamed "Oh my God!" and we stopped so I could run to a pay phone to call Cleve. But he didn't pick up. We headed for city hall, where a huge crowd had already gathered. Everyone looked dazed, holding their hands to their heads. City hall was cordoned off, ambulances parked at the side entrance. It dawned on me: This was really happening. Harvey had been assassinated.

I met up with Cleve at a big candlelight march that night. We hugged and cried, but inside our hearts a fire burned. We understood there was a coup going on. Our enemies were real and they wanted us dead. It was rumored that Milk's assassin, former supervisor Dan White, gave himself up for arrest only after he spoke with the politically powerful elders at St. Mary's Cathedral. What we had won at the ballot box they could take away with their bullets. It was so horrible, we could do nothing for days but weep. Harvey's life was gone, and so were our dreams.

Winter was coming and I wanted to crawl into a cocoon. Morgan and I hibernated together in his Victorian flat on Pine Street and examined various conspiracy theories that suggested a link between White's murders and the support of the local Catholic archdiocese and the city's police and fire departments. Some people claimed that even Mayor Moscone's successor, Dianne Feinstein, was involved.

When Dan White was found guilty only of manslaughter on May 21, 1979, we were shocked but not surprised. He would receive the lightest possible sentence for a man convicted of killing two people. Morgan called the situation "a holy war between the cops and the queers." Cleve said, "This is the final straw; the courts are covering up the assassination as a final bullet to the heart of the lesbian and gay liberation movement." He said we should go down to city hall.

When we got there, a riot was going on. Rage was the only thing left to feel. People were burning police cars and breaking all the windows in the building, trying to set it on fire. They ripped the ornamental grillwork from the front doors and rammed the huge iron and brass pieces through the beveled glass. I remembered the old '60s saying, "If you can't change it, burn it down." Police chased us away with clubs in their hands. Later, cops came down to Castro Street and stormed the Elephant Walk bar, Harvey's favorite, and beat up all the customers in retaliation.

Cleve got blamed for the rioting that evening and was summoned to a grand jury looking into who incited it. He wasn't charged, but now he had a reputation as the city's official gay troublemaker. Mayor Feinstein hated him, the police despised him, and the gay establishment disowned him.

There was a holy war going on, and the gay community was losing it. Holy wars were very "in" during the spring of 1979. The Ayatollah Khomeini was instituting a jihad in Iran that was killing off its own people, many of them because they were gay. Preachers in American pulpits endorsed the idea that violence committed against homosexuals was morally justified. One night, Morgan and I got attacked by a gang when we walked home from the movies. There were so many young kids shouting, "Kill the fags!" They bloodied up our faces before we managed to get away. We had to run for our lives. And when Morgan went to make a police report, the cops laughed at him.

With Harvey's death, it seemed the unity he had inspired died along with him. The lesbian and gay community ruptured into competing factions. In light of Dan White's lenient verdict and the subsequent "White Night" riot, it seemed rather odd to start planning the 1979 Gay Freedom Day Parade. There wasn't anything to celebrate, and there was plenty to protest.

But I remembered what Harvey had said about giving them hope. I planned to sew up hundreds of new Rainbow Flags to make the event colorful at a time when everybody was ready to paint it black. I wanted to show the world we would survive.

7

Raining on My Parade

I called up Walter Caplan, who was working on the new Gay Freedom Day Committee, recently organized as an independent nonprofit corporation. I wanted to share my plan to create a city landscape of Rainbow Flags for the 1979 parade. I led him on a walk along Market Street, explaining how the project might look. I told him about my plan to get funding for it. The old parade committee, under the auspices of the Pride Foundation, was about to receive $10,000 from the city—a grant to reimburse the group for past expenses. It was required to spend that money on the 1979 parade. I suggested to Walter that the Pride Foundation might be willing to fund the Rainbow Flags, since it was never going to give the money to the new nonprofit committee.

Walter liked the idea of flags, but he was cool on the idea of using the ten thousand. He wanted that money to go to his new nonprofit corporation. Despite Walter's misgivings, a couple of days later I went up to the Pride Foundation offices in the Gay Community Center and pitched the flag project. Since I had a reputation for being crazy, the board asked a few questions. Then they talked among themselves and voted to support me. Once again, I went happily skipping down the old wooden staircase. We would install four hundred Rainbow Flags from one end of town to the other during Gay Freedom Day.

There wasn't any way to construct that many banners in the workshop at the Gay Community Center, so I called up Paramount Flag

Company to see if they would manufacture them. They invited me to come over.

At the time, I had been at a fashion shoot, helping my old friend Robert Opel. When I arrived at the flag factory, I was wearing pink lamé jeans and a chartreuse leopard skin tank top. My hair was chopped off and dyed orange. I looked fabulous. But what happened at Paramount was even more fabulous.

A cherubic young man met me at the top of the stairs and introduced himself as Jim Ferrigan. He remembered putting the grommets in the handmade flag that we had rushed in for emergency repair in 1978. He wanted to know what the Rainbow Flag was all about. I told him about its role as a symbol for the lesbian and gay rights movement. Jim was intrigued. He ushered me into a back office to meet the vice president who would handle the arrangements. We shook hands. Ken Hughes was handsome, I thought; he had reddish hair and a short beard. He looked me up one side and down the other, taking in my pink lamé and leopard skin, as if evaluating my sanity.

I told Ken that we wanted four hundred flags and hardware attachments that would fit the Market Street lampposts. I wanted them in the same original eight colors as the first flags in 1978, but Ken explained that it would be too expensive. We finally settled on six stripes: primary colors red, yellow, and blue, and secondary colors orange, green, and purple. Ken suggested creating them in nylon, a material more durable for outdoor use. He had an assistant type up an invoice for $7,000. Then he gave me a tour around the factory. There was a big silk-screen printing setup on the first floor, and women were sewing on the second floor. It was amazing. I had never considered flag-making to be much of an enterprise, but it was clear that something big was happening here. Every wall was covered with posters and paintings. Huge cabinets displayed china and tchotchkes. The whole place was filled with all sorts of flag memorabilia. It was a museum for the industrial art of flag-making.

The next day, I brought Ken a check from the Pride Foundation. Both he and Jim were surprised that I'd acted so quickly, and equally impressed with my knowledge of sewing. They invited me to watch the construction of the Rainbow Flags.

The next morning, I went down to Paramount. Huge bolts of fabric were brought up from the basement to be cut. The project was under-way, and I watched in complete fascination.

But my joy didn't last for long. I was soon summoned to Ken's office. There was a big problem. The bank had called; a lawsuit had been filed the day before by the new parade committee's nonprofit, and the Pride Foundation's bank account had been frozen by a temporary restraining order. Their check to Paramount was no good.

I was dumbstruck. Ken was mad. The fabric had already been cut up, and I was financially responsible. *Did I have $7,000?* Ken wanted to know. I felt sick, but I promised him I would find out what was going on. Ken's steel-blue eyes weren't smiling. I figured this straight businessman felt the gay community was a joke and he had just been screwed by a drag queen. That bothered me; I wanted him to like me. We shook hands and I was off to find a lawyer to handle this mess.

The only lawyer I knew besides Walter Caplan (who was repre-senting the parade committee nonprofit in the case) was Mark Rennie. Walter had introduced me to Mark in 1978 when we raised the first flag. Mark was also a photographer who lived a few doors down from Robert Opel's storefront gallery Fey-Way Studios on Howard Street. When I told Mark my predicament, he immediately agreed to represent me. Soon, his assistant drafted a press release to notify the media of our side of the story. We had to work fast; Channel 4 was already over at the flag factory.

Mark connected with Paramount's attorneys at Dinkelspiel & Dinkelspiel. Then they both got on the horn with the Pride Founda-tion attorneys, led by John Wahl. Walter got attorney Tom Steele to represent the Gay Freedom Day Committee nonprofit. The hearing would be in superior court the very next day.

The next morning, Mark escorted me into the courtroom on the third floor of city hall. Following his advice, I was wearing blue jeans and a white T-shirt. "You're the artist," he had instructed me, "so you should look like Andy Warhol." His final instructions as we walked in? "Just look at the judge and look sad."

So I just kept looking at the judge sadly. He would look down from the big oak bench and smile at me in return. The attorneys were called up one by one to explain themselves. The judge listened. It was over in less than five minutes. His verdict: the money belonged to the Pride Foundation—they could do what they wanted with it. And spending it for the beautification of the city was a noble solution, he added. I thanked him. I went back to Paramount and Ken gave me a kiss. I didn't know what to think.

We completed the installation of the Rainbow Flags in late June, a few days before the parade. We ended up having to use tall, rickety ladders to get them up along Market Street. The flags were beautiful and attracted wide attention and praise.

We also hung up Faerie's magnificent 1978 flag with the field of tie-dyed stars on the exterior of the Gay Community Center. But it soon disappeared. We were told that some workmen from the new symphony hall going up across the street had probably taken it. We went over to see. They were pouring concrete down into a big hole. They wouldn't talk to us and threw us out. I wondered if they might be burying the evidence right in front of us. Faerie was so disillusioned that she moved to Japan two weeks later.

It rained on the 1979 Gay Freedom Day Parade. San Francisco was a soggy, sorry mess. When the parade was over later that afternoon, we walked around the Civic Center to take down the flags. But the parade committee people would not let us; members grabbed them from us. When I protested, somebody punched me and knocked me out. When I came to, on the muddy ground, I saw people all around me, hitting each other and screaming obscenities. They were fighting over the Rainbow Flags, pulling on them like a game of tug-of-war, tearing them.

It was over, I thought. The end of the lesbian and gay movement. A year to the day after we had created the Rainbow Flag, people were now beating each other up over ownership of a piece of cloth. We were supposed to be giving the world hope, not an orgy of hate and infighting. The ideas behind the Rainbow Flag seemed to have been forgotten. I decided it was a failure as a symbol—just another flag for people to fight over.

8

Life at the Clown Hotel

Lawyer Mark Rennie was the leading advocate for public art in San Francisco; he had organized massive exhibitions on billboards and the sides of buildings. Mark had just purchased a dilapidated transient hotel to provide artist housing. We called it the Clown Hotel, because some of the tenants were mimes that he managed. Mark's boyfriend was a member of the troupe, which performed for tourists at Fisherman's Wharf. The Clown Hotel was at the corner of Ninth and Folsom Streets in the South of Market neighborhood. This once-isolated industrial area was emerging as ground zero for the city's burgeoning art scene and was home to several popular gay leather bars. Mark offered me an apartment at the Clown Hotel in return for helping on renovations. I moved in and began knocking out walls between the tiny rooms and refinishing the wood floors.

After the crushing embarrassment of the mud fight at the 1979 Gay Freedom Day Parade, I needed to find another channel for my political activism. Mark encouraged me to explore theater as a constructive laboratory for my interest in symbolism and satire. In the Clown Hotel was a sewing room and another room for dressing. Mark got me a gig outfitting his Fisherman's Wharf mimes. I got serious about making costumes.

The hotel was just around the corner from Mark's loft and Robert Opel's Fey-Way Studios. The seedy glamour of the neighborhood

One of Gilbert's mime costumes, a custom-made tuxedo worn by Rainbow the Mime as he performs for tourists.

Photo by Judy Parker, from the collection of Mark Rennie

attracted a wave of new settlers. Paramount Flag was one block south on Ninth Street, one of the few local manufacturers left. The others had left long ago for the suburbs. There was a desolation and decay here that seemed sexy. I didn't have a boyfriend, and the streets at two thirty in the morning were full of handsome men looking for action.

One night, around the witching hour, I thought to go over to Fey-Way, where there was sure to be a party. Robert had adopted me as an artist and periodically gave me money to buy art supplies. He was also a performance artist before the term became popular. In 1974, pursuing the fad known as "streaking," he made international headlines by running nude through the Oscars ceremony. For the 1979 Freedom Day Parade, he reenacted the assassination of Harvey Milk, going so far as to find a leather guy who was the spitting image of Dan White. It was so outrageous, people from the parade committee panicked and placed their hands over TV cameras to keep them from recording the scene.

Robert had also funded a silk-screened protest poster I made for Freedom Day. It showed the city hall dome coming off and the message Don't Stop the Rainbow. I wanted to take him a special copy. As I approached the gallery, Ruby Zebra, a poet who lived across from the Clown Hotel, was running toward me. There were a lot of cops at Fey-Way, he said. I wondered if Robert had been busted for drugs—a logical concern, since he was frequently using drugs of every kind. Soon Mark Rennie appeared, white with shock. Robert had been shot dead in a robbery.

The police searched the gallery and found drugs and what the newspapers described as pornography—actually, a series of art photographs by Robert Mapplethorpe. The cops also suggested this was a drug deal gone wrong. We wondered if the cops were dealing drugs and might have been pushing speed to Robert. A few days later, the family arrived and packed up the art collection—a vast array of erotic gay art, including paintings, drawings, sculptures, and photographs. They closed the gallery, padlocked the doors, and left town.

Robert's death had a sobering effect on my life, like Harvey Milk's assassination. Both had been fighting for the rights of the individual against the oppression of the state. Robert's life had involved sexuality and drugs. He had crusaded for our freedom to enjoy both. Sex and drugs are the same struggle, because they challenge authority with the power of choice. After their deaths, I felt lost.

At night alone in bed, I thought about our struggle. It wasn't going to be a pretty garden-party sexual revolution in which justice for lesbians and gays would be won gracefully. I knew we were in for a long and bloody battle. They had the guns. Did we have the faith and courage?

San Francisco's spirit of freedom included the freedom to use drugs. It was a city where little cable cars, stoned halfway to the stars, operated under a Victorian skyline of smokestacks churning up a cloud of marijuana smoke. Pot was always my favorite high. Everyone I knew smoked it. People were very open about it. When we walked down Castro Street on Sunday afternoons, we would toke up right on the street. Though the 1972 marijuana initiative, Proposition 19, had failed, my friend Dennis Peron was building a new movement for legalization. In 1978, with the help of Harvey Milk, he had put a measure in front of the San Francisco electorate to demand that the authorities stop arresting and prosecuting marijuana offenses. It won handily, though it had no force of law.

If you were a gay man in San Francisco during the '70s, drugs were part of your life. Bars and discos were where you went. You brought illegal drugs with you and mixed them with alcohol. This cocktail of energy was the daily bread of an entire community. I had experimented with drugs since my days at the Presidio in 1970. By the end of the decade, I had tried everything. Shortly before Robert's murder, I experimented with heroin and cocaine. Amphetamines and barbiturates were everywhere, and I considered them to be entertaining but too pharmaceutical to provide enlightenment. My taste leaned toward the total psychedelic experience. I liked LSD and psilocybin mushrooms. Peyote took me on a trip that lasted three days. But as the years went on, people were overdoing it, getting sick and strung out. I rarely drank alcohol and attributed the wave of burnout and exotic illnesses to the ravages of the bottle.

From my window at the Clown Hotel, I could look down the street to Paramount Flag. There were always colorful flags flying from the rooftop. One afternoon, I went over there to see about making more Rainbow Flags. Ken Hughes introduced me to the owner, John Tuteur. He was a very spry gentleman, well into his later years, who amused himself by collecting flag memorabilia. Ken told me that flagmakers were formally called vexillographers, as vexillography is the art of designing symbols and flags.

We went into the basement, where they kept all the stuff left from jobs over the past sixty years. The placed looked Victorian. It was amazing. Jim Ferrigan enthusiastically offered scholarly facts about every flag. I was intrigued by the possibilities.

I really liked red-haired Ken Hughes. After that kiss from him, I wondered if he was really as straight as he looked. So I took a chance and asked him for a date. Ken accepted, then laughed at the look of relief on my face. He had assumed that I knew he was gay. We made a date to go to the beach.

That afternoon, the Pacific Ocean was in a mist. We huddled together against the seawall. I reached out to touch him. We put our arms around each other, letting the wind blow its watery dew across our faces. Later that night, I looked at his chiseled face and lost myself in his silvery-blue eyes. Under his plaid shirt beat the heart of a great romantic and adventurer. Ken turned me on with his soul and passion for understanding. We made out until midnight.

Later, Ken drove me home. I stuffed my hard-on down in my jeans when we pulled up in front of the Clown Hotel. We would continue to love each other, but ultimately we would keep it as friends. Ken was more than a muse; he was an angel. He would teach me many things. Yet after twenty years of knowing him, my dick would still be throbbing.

The next time Ken and I got together, I asked him for a job. I wanted to design and build window displays for the Flag Store, Paramount's retail shop on Polk Street. We agreed that they would supply all the materials and I would get twenty-five dollars for each display I created. A few days later, I was turned loose in the flag factory.

Industrial sewing was a new world. The women who worked at Paramount took interest in my sewing, even as they pitied my unskilled methods. Miriam, Susie, and Gladys taught me how to do graphic appliqué. Fay Lee gave me instruction on operating industrial sewing machines. The hours and hours of handiwork that went into creating flags was considerable. I started to appreciate flag-making as a fine art.

For Christmas, I turned the whole Polk Street storefront into one giant display, centered around the theme "At Home with Betsy Ross and Santa Claus." Everything was made in the motif of the stars and stripes, and we complemented them with wonderful objects from Mr. Tuteur's basement collection of antique memorabilia. Tourists flocked to the Flag Store.

Flag-flying was suddenly a very "in" thing to do. It seemed a little weird. The passion was connected to the excesses of phony patriotism coming out of the Republican Party leading up to the 1980 presidential election. Thanks to Ronald Reagan, American flags were flying off the shelves. But I noticed something else too: more and more people were now asking for the Rainbow Flag on a daily basis. Within two months, we had exhausted the entire supply of domestic purple cotton bunting. Soon, other manufacturers got interested in making Rainbow Flags. We had to switch over from cotton to nylon to keep up with the demand.

Somehow this idea of mine, born in a moment of bliss on the dance floor, was growing, taking on a life of its own in a way that surprised even me.

When I wasn't creating flags, I was hanging out with my new friend, Tom Taylor. He was a carpenter, electrician, welder, cabinetmaker, plumber, roofer, structural engineer, and hairdresser. We had met at a parade committee meeting. He hated it and never came back; he preferred to help make things for the movement, not create policy. Tom hired me for his workshop on Clementina Street.

I helped him design and build straight strip joints. He showed me how to use power tools. I finally was in a shop class, having avoided it in high school. We worked long hours, constructing all sorts of fantastic special effects for topless girls on nightclub catwalks, including tacky props. Excess was the fashion of the times, and who could do it better than two butch queens? We worked steel, brocade, and a few lasers into the sets for a straight man's most erotic fantasy. We could make anything. One day it would be velvet stage drapes on an electrical track. The next day, we cut up black Formica and PVC to give a ceiling a Pullman train car look in leather and brass. I also used my new skills to construct elaborate mechanical displays for the Flag Store.

Tom's boyfriend Jerry Goldstein was a doctor. He and his friends, mostly other gay doctors, organized the Bay Area Physicians for Human Rights to support pro-gay legislation. I discovered that rich gay doctors were behind much of the blossoming movement. In 1979, many of them were already worried about the developing conservative backlash.

Tom put together fabulous parties to raise funds and attract supporters. I began to help him, and I got to see how the other half lived.

I was surviving, barely. Cleve complained that I was too skinny. He made weekend dinners for me. Everyone around me seemed to be going to the doctor and the clinic for the clap or syphilis. Then came a rise in hepatitis, and all sorts of exotic parasites. It meant taking lots of pills and keeping calendars for when it was safe to have sex again. Even Morgan, the strongest and most handsome guy I knew, became infected.

Meanwhile, President Jimmy Carter was being pilloried as a coward for allowing Americans to be taken hostage by Iran during the explosion of anti-American terrorism that accompanied the country's Islamic revolution. The takeover in Iran by Muslim fundamentalists fascinated me. I followed the whole drama from the fall of the shah through the return of the Ayatollah Khomeini and then the taking of hostages. Every night, ABC News tracked the crisis. We watched as a new number would appear, superimposed over the flags of the United States and Iran, announcing the number of days the hostages had been held.

Morgan told me he was thinking of voting for Ronald Reagan, reasoning that he couldn't be worse than Jimmy Carter. Cleve thought he was crazy. I didn't like Ronald Reagan. He had been elected governor twice in California, to everyone's consternation. Now he was running for president. I watched him campaigning at Christian colleges with TV preachers like Jerry Falwell. In a way, the theocratic revolution going on in Iran had parallels in America—even in San Francisco. It bothered me.

The left was splitting, with President Carter being challenged in the Democratic primaries by Senator Ted Kennedy. George Bush, Mr. CIA himself, was challenging Reagan for the Republican nomination, and there was still that big silent majority from Nixon's era who had to weigh in. But when Morgan changed his vote, I realized Reagan would win. We were in for it.

9

The Birth of
Sister Chanel 2001

Morgan and I had heard about a group of drag queens in Haight-Ashbury throwing a New Year's Eve party in a big dance studio. They dressed as nuns and called themselves the Sisters of Perpetual Indulgence. This was guerrilla street theater at its most politically extreme. This carnival of blasphemy had one major target: the anti-gay hierarchy of the Catholic Church. The whole thrust was to throw light on Christian oppression in public life—the wave of homophobia currently coming out of the Vatican and from TV's evangelical preachers. It seemed audacious, attacking Christianity, but it was the source of centuries of oppression. I believed that Jesus, who preached love and acceptance, might have been gay.

Everything about the Sisters was a parody of religion, from the way they dressed to their Sunday meetings at their "convent." Some of them had actually been in seminary, and many were ex-Catholics. Satire and humor were the best weapons they had against the guns and hatred of those who called themselves Christian. The Sisters of Perpetual Indulgence were on a mission to expiate stigmatic guilt and spread universal joy—while pushing the buttons of the pious. They were true clowns and media marauders, straight out of the French Revolution. There was something magnificent and terrible about them, visually and symbolically.

I took Morgan as my date to the Sisters' party. He wore a pink tuxedo I had made him for Christmas. I wore a silver sequined jumpsuit with a matching beaded headdress. We ran into pot crusader Dennis Peron. Poet James Broughton read his masterpiece "Hermes." We toasted the beginning of the '80s, dancing till dawn. This strange order of drag nuns was irresistible fun. I saw the possibilities for making costumes for them. I chatted up one of the nuns, Sister Missionary Position. "Sister Mish," as the inner circle called her, and I exchanged phone numbers.

The popularity of Rainbow Flags continued to rise in 1980. They were suddenly everywhere. I saw them flying from houses in the Castro, and then merchants began to put them up on storefronts. It seemed this symbolic visibility was working; gay tourists would stream into the Flag Store and buy them. For many, this purchase was a coming-out, telling the world who they were. Paramount decided to order up five thousand more. Mark Rennie was disappointed that no patent or copyright could be issued, as all flag designs are in the public domain. It didn't bother me. In fact, that was the whole point of creating it. I liked the idea of the Rainbow Flag not belonging to any one individual and the fact that anyone could do anything with it.

Straight tourists would come into the store, many of them flag and history buffs. They were drawn to the colorful flag they saw on every street. Jim Ferrigan, who was straight, would tell them it was the flag of the gay community. He would patiently explain to these alien beings in polyester the story of the struggle for lesbian and gay civil liberties. After listening politely, the tourists would quickly head to the other part of the store for an American flag.

I was depressed when Ronald Reagan was elected president in November 1980. When John Lennon was murdered in front of the Dakota in New York City only five weeks later, it made me crazy. America was out to kill any messenger of peace and love. People worshipped the stars and stripes with the same fervor they had for the cross. I began noticing the connection. In one of the books in Jim Ferrigan's office, I read where patriotism is the last refuge of scoundrels. America under Reagan was becoming a place of empty nationalism. It was Rome under Caesar, full of TV circuses, masquerades of wealth, and cruel righteousness.

In response, I started making outrageous drag getups out of American flags. I would dress up like allegorical Greek goddesses or Miss Liberty and go visit with the Sisters of Perpetual Indulgence at their convent on Ashbury Street. Sister Mish lived there with the Reverend Mother, and they introduced me to Sister Mary Media and Sister Loganberry Frost, who lived around the corner at Babylon, another drag commune.

One night, I had my chance to show the sisters what I could do. It was a protest against the Salvadoran Civil War, in which the military government, backed by the United States, was systematically killing the opposition, a coalition of left-wing groups. I dressed everyone in the flags of Latin America, each one worn like a strapless sheath, with ghoulish makeup and coffin hairdos. We went to Polk Street and crashed a Christian missionary rally against gays, performing a "death squad beauty pageant." We lit firecrackers and waved cardboard machine guns.

Now I was part of the group. We would regularly dress up in convent drag and go out for a walk in the Haight or the Castro. We were shocking and provocative, both beating away the camera-toting tourists and coming on to them.

When the Catholic archdiocese canceled a performance of the Gay Men's Chorus at the Jesuit-run University of San Francisco, Sister Mish led a protest of hundreds in front of St. Ignatius Church on campus. The archdiocese denounced the Sisters as morally depraved trouble-makers who gave the gay community a bad name. This got Cleve off the hook; he now looked reasonable, even respectable, next to Sister Boom Boom waving a dildo at tourists.

Sister Mish and Reverend Mother took me under their wing and hooked me up with Sister Hysterectoria, Agnes de Garron, who was pure show biz in the old tradition. There was an exacting process to officially become a Sister of Perpetual Indulgence. First you were a novice, required to work on three events and wear a white veil. Black veils were reserved for fully professed sisters who had taken vows at a special investiture ceremony.

Male drag nuns seemed almost the opposite of the Rainbow Flag. A black-and-white clutter, instead of simple color. A tactic of confrontation, rather than a celebration of beauty as a means of visibility. The Rainbow Flag and the Sisters of Perpetual Indulgence were, in many ways, the sacred and profane symbols of the same struggle. We started doing appearances every day. It was a full-time drag revolution. My imagination took off.

I became Sister Chanel 2001, after the French designer and the Kubrick sci-fi movie classic. I bought fifty yards of white bridal veil and black taffeta and prepared for my instruction as a novice. But my participation was controversial; some sisters considered me a media opportunist, too spiritually lightweight for the task at hand. But after my sufficient period of subservient humility and service, I was finally approved to be a Sister.

My first required appearance began when Sister Boom Boom and Sister Krishna Kosher planned a rally at Union Square. I created a copy of Princess Diana's wedding gown—in black. Our job was to upstage a Christian fundamentalist revival going on in the little park, held by a group called S.O.S.—Save Our Souls—who said that San Francisco had become Sodom and Gomorrah. It was a common theme among the fundies; TV preacher Jerry Falwell had called our city a golden gateway to hell.

Twenty minutes after we arrived, the S.O.S. revival was in shambles. Sister Boom Boom, dressed up like a lion in chains and carrying a whip, was threatening to eat the Christians, saying so in a very sexual tone. Sister Hysterectoria and Reverend Mother gathered the counterprotesters into a circle. They held hands and extended around the entire block. We now had the S.O.S. people surrounded. The police tac squad was called out, but how could they arrest people for merely dancing? We stayed until the fundies gave up, and we all sang the "Hallelujah" chorus as they quickly fled back to the suburbs.

There was also infighting among the sisters—an ongoing debate about whether to officially organize the group, as opposed to allowing anarchy in high heels. A meeting was called to determine what kind of organization we would be. One faction wanted to become a professional theatrical troupe. The other, a traditional charitable organization. The votes were counted. The verdict: the Sisters of Perpetual Indulgence would form themselves as a not-for-profit corporation. We had decided to go legit.

Mayor Dianne Feinstein had attended Catholic girls' school in San Francisco, and she did not think the idea of drag nuns waving dildos at tourists was good for the city's image, making San Francisco the Kook Capital of the World. Feinstein wanted an explanation and summoned Sister Mish to her lavish offices in city hall—where, only a few years earlier, Mayor George Moscone had been murdered.

Sister Mish attended the summit wearing the regulation wimple—called the ear brassiere—accented by a hoop skirt and full nun regalia. Feinstein took one look at her guest and got mad. She was not going to tolerate obscenity. The mayor stressed to Mish that she saw red every time the Sisters appeared in the paper. She demanded we clean up our act.

Sister Mish returned to the convent and recounted the tense meeting, especially the mayor's quote about our media coverage, adding, "If the mayor wants to see red, we'll give it to her."

I was assigned to produce and direct an event we called the Red Party. It would be a satirical send-up of Communism, since the mayor considered us a Bolshevik nightmare. Russians were in the news at the time. Ronald Reagan was talking about the evil Soviet empire, spinning his version of a Red Scare into a moral crusade. Meanwhile, Warren Beatty and Diane Keaton were in the historical film *Reds*, burning up the silver screen with their love story of American Communists John Reed and Louise Bryant. I went to see the movie several times with Reverend Mother and bought the soundtrack album. It had a recording of the "Internationale" by the Moscow Radio Chorus. It was very solemn and slow, so we rerecorded it sped up. The "Internationale" became our theme music as we started rehearsing our performances for the Red Party.

We needed a party venue. I remembered an old Victorian building on Sutter Street in the Fillmore neighborhood called the Russian Center. You could rent it for events. Reverend Mother and I went over to look at it. The whole place was done up in red-and-gold flocked wallpaper and wood paneling. It was filled with '50s vinyl and Formica furniture covered in plastic lace. The architecture was slightly Romanesque. The Russian Center would not have looked out of place in Red Square. The center's large ballroom had a beautiful oak dance floor and included a stage with a gilt proscenium and heavy red drapes. A balcony mezzanine wrapped around over our heads. It was fabulous and could accommodate at least a thousand people

We filled out forms, paid the deposit, and reserved our date. We intentionally chose Saturday, May 1, 1982, the date of the annual Russian public holiday called Day of the International Solidarity of Workers.

We spent two days unloading the lights and sound equipment into the old building. It was more like a rock show or circus. Miles of heavy cables were strung. We had to get a special hookup from Pacific Gas & Electric to facilitate so much electricity pouring into the place. There were huge trucks full of props and costumes, catering and booze. It was hard work, sweat, and glitter. We had grease under our press-on nails.

Then one day, I was having scrambled eggs at the Norse Cove diner on Castro Street. From the window, I watched a white Peterbilt truck come around the corner, hauling a white rocket. I ran out and waved the driver to a stop. He called his metal rocket the Elvis. This daredevil planned to shoot himself across the bay. The guy was a real nut, but he agreed to rent his rocket for our party.

The morning of the Red Party, I woke up around six in the morning and stumbled over to the Russian Center. The newsstand headlines screamed, War Declared. Margaret Thatcher had sent the Royal Navy to take back the Falkland Islands from Argentina. Not such a great way to start this event. The Elvis appeared right on time at 7:00 AM, early enough to park right in front of the Russian Center. The daredevil activated a hydraulic lift to raise the rocket into an erect state. An elderly neighbor suddenly approached us. She didn't think putting a missile in front of the Russian Center was a good idea.

Reverend Mother appeared in one of the upper windows and began hanging the giant red buntings we had sewn together, as well as red flags from the USSR and the People's Republic of China, rented from the Flag Store. I'd crafted hammers and sickles from plywood, covered in gold glitter.

The notorious Elvis rocket that Gilbert hired for the Sisters of Perpetual Indulgence's scandalous Red Party. *Photo by Ian Malloy, courtesy of the Australian Lesbian and Gay Archives*

The elderly neighbor reappeared, even madder. She wanted to know if the people from the center knew what was going on. We assured her everything was just fine. But when I mentioned a performance by the Sisters of Perpetual Indulgence, her eyes narrowed. She went back to her house and stationed herself at her window with a phone in her hand. The police soon came. But the rocket was parked legally and we had a permit for our sound system. They left.

When the sun went down, big trucks with authentic Hollywood klieg lights were turned on and lit up the twilight. The daredevil had sparks in his eyes when he saw the Elvis in the glow of a million watts.

At eight o'clock, the overture began. I went backstage to change from dirty blue jeans to a silver sequined sheath in the style of the Virgin Mary. All of the sisters would make an appearance center stage in their special gowns and red habits for a pageant. Using a broom closet as a dressing room, I started pulling my clothes off. Morgan was guarding the door while Tede Matthews and Mary Media were slapping makeup on my face. We could hear the floor shaking from the stomping and thunderous applause as the pageant began.

Suddenly, Sister Mish appeared at the broom closet door. She told me to follow her downstairs, where I came face to face with very indignant people led by the old neighbor lady. They gawked at me. I realized I wasn't wearing a shirt, and that my face was covered with makeup. They all started talking at once, saying we had to close down right now. Some said they were from the Russian Center. We were disturbing the peace, so our hall rental contract was terminated. They especially objected to the flags on the front of the building and the Soviet symbols. They were White Russians, not Communists, they said, and accused us of being commie infiltrators.

I pulled the contract from my back pocket and calmly told them the show had already started. Sister Mish graciously explained, like a queen in her personal salon, that there was really nothing to be done. As the intruders began getting pushy with Mish, my patience evaporated. I exploded, "If you don't like it, you can sue us! And if you try to close us down, we will sue you!" These people had picked a fight with the wrong drag queens. I pulled some liquid black eyeliner from my jeans pocket, unscrewed the applicator, and pointed it at them, and admonished them to either go home or come inside and watch the show. I turned around and went back to the dressing room.

I had already missed my cue and Sister CPR was bringing the house down in a shower of silver and red light. The show was a sensation. I went up to the balcony to the mix boards and tried to calm down. I saw the Russian delegation come in and huddle in a corner. Sister Mish, the peacemaker, told me she thought it would be a good idea if we took the flags off the front of the building. These Russian Center people were crazy enough to really sue, and we could not afford a lawsuit; the Red Party was only breaking even. A poll of the other sisters decided we should take down the Communist flags and hammers and sickles but leave the rest up. Mish went to take care of it.

When Reverend Mother took the stage, alone in a blue spotlight, the whole room was bathed in a satanic red. The faces of the Russian delegation were in shock. But when the sisters came on for the finale, dancing to the sped-up "Internationale," the Russians finally laughed, getting the joke.

The Russians didn't sue us, but they did smear us in the newspapers for insulting them—and for leaving lipstick on the walls of the men's room. The Red Party became legendary after that; we won the Cable Car Award for most outstanding special event of the year.

But the infamous party had lingering effects. In 1990, Soviet leader Mikhail Gorbachev was coming to visit San Francisco. The Berlin Wall, the international symbol of Communism, had come tumbling down the previous year. By this point, I had already designed special events for several heads of state, including the premier of the People's Republic of China and President Mitterrand of France. But I was not called to participate in the festivities for Gorby. I presumed that the Soviets had heard of our Red Party and didn't want their people mixing with homosexuals.

A year after Gorby came to San Francisco, he was history. So was the Soviet Union. The red flag of Russia, which had provoked so much fear and hysteria, was replaced on government buildings by the tricolored banner that had preceded the Communist flag.

A while after the Red Party, I was talking with Morgan about the backlash toward flags, both Rainbow and Russian. Flying flags is a means of self-expression. But sometimes that action makes you the target. In 1982, I was just starting to discover how much.

"It had to happen," Morgan said about the backlash. He also pointed out that the street theater of the Sisters of Perpetual Indulgence no longer had the same impact. "People have bigger things on their minds than the Church," he said.

"Like what, politics?"

"Death," Morgan replied. "People are thinking about death. Nobody gives a fuck about some illusion of a movement. The only revolution going on is Reagan's."

I disagreed. "We have more power now than ever. Reagan hasn't stopped us."

"You don't get it," Morgan insisted. "Because you don't have it." He paused, shook his head in disgust, and continued. "I have it." He said it again, almost like some part of him did not believe it. "I've got it."

He was talking about the new cancer that was striking only gay men.

I could see tears in Morgan's eyes. I gasped for air. "God, I'm so sorry," I said, but the words didn't seem sufficient. I reached out to him. Morgan collapsed into me. "You're the first to know," he said, sobbing on my shoulder. "What will I tell my parents? They don't even know I'm gay."

"Don't worry," I said, patting his back. "Everything will be OK."

I knew I was lying.

10

Bobbi Took Off His Socks

It was the spring of 1982. I was sitting in the big bay window of the apartment that looked out over Golden Gate Park. I was with Bobbi Campbell, my new roommate. He had recently moved into the attic bedroom of "the Brain Trust," a drag commune around the corner from the Sisters of Perpetual Indulgence convent. Bobbi was a novice and worked with great enthusiasm on every assignment. He had been involved with the Red Party. Bobbi was a registered nurse at the University of California Medical Center, so he'd taken the name Sister Florence Nightmare, RN.

Bobbi asked me if I had heard of GRID. The acronym stood for gay-related immune deficiency, the current name for the gay cancer that everyone seemed to be getting. He knew that I had some interest in nursing and medicine from my days as a US Army medic.

Bobbi took off his shoes and socks and showed me purple spots on his slender feet. These were cancerous lesions, he explained, called Kaposi's sarcoma, a symptom of GRID. Looking like sharp bruises, they continued up his ankles and disappeared under his blue jeans. I asked Bobbi if the lesions hurt. He said he was on chemotherapy to treat them.

I had heard people saying GRID was on the verge of becoming an epidemic. Cleve and Bobbi were putting together a KS Foundation with one of the UC Medical doctors, Marcus Conant.

We sat watching the traffic below slide past our lace curtains. Bobbi told me he felt called spiritually to become a Sister of Perpetual Indulgence. "A great epidemic is coming. It's like germ warfare or something. Only gay people are getting this. It's genocide. This is not an accident; this is happening to us. We are going to have to fight for our lives." He was serious. There was a very clear white light in Bobbi's eyes. I could see he knew he was dying. It was frightening to think of the enormity of what lay ahead. I wondered if we would all die.

I remembered from my army days the secret biological warfare laboratories at Letterman General Hospital and how suddenly they expanded in 1971, moving into a giant new building. The word was they made Agent Orange there and they were making new stuff. I'd even taken part in classified experiments in which they shot dogs with X-rays to see what radiation would do to them and had us study the results. In an operating theater, we would cut open the poor little specimens with scalpels and then suture up their wounds with surgical needles and thread. Gruesome. I told Bobbi all this.

It didn't seem far-fetched to imagine these same people had cooked up a solution to deal with gay liberation. After all, Nixon had been in New York City the weekend of the Stonewall riots. He was the new president then, only in office since January. He had been elected on a platform of law and order. A riot of drag queens and homosexuals certainly would have attracted Nixon's attention.

Bobbi was so brazen and sincere. He excited me because he wanted to fight back. He put on some old Motown records and we danced around the living room and in the big hallway. Bobbi spun me into his arms, since he knew all the steps. He wanted to take over the Sisters and use them as a channel of communicating about the impending biological holocaust. He was very up front with his agenda. The Sisters, he said, had established themselves as the high authority on sex. "We have to talk about it and tell people how to fuck safely."

Fuck safely? I didn't understand. Getting fucked in the ass was already risky enough with all the syphilis going around. Fisting was very popular, but not for me.

After Bobbi talked to me that day, I began to agree with him that GRID was genocide. My old army hospital experience had previously been my armor against the epidemic. I used to look at GRID medically, emotionally detached. But after seeing Bobbi's KS, I couldn't detach anymore; besides, I had several friends passing away.

Morgan was more than a friend with GRID; he was someone I loved. He had lost fifty pounds in less than a month. His vast wardrobe was now useless; nothing fit. A few weeks after he told me his diagnosis, we went out for a picnic at the Palace of Fine Arts. In my army medic days, I used to escape the tortures of the Presidio and skip up the street made of stairs. Morgan was self-conscious about walking over the crest of Pacific Heights to the monument, due to shaky legs and the fear that his trousers, now too big, would fall down. So I helped thread a rope through his loops and tied it to secure his pants. Now, Morgan made his way more confidently to the Lyon Street steps and Broadway.

Morgan loved to walk through the exclusive neighborhood that crowns the hilltop. The richest people in San Francisco lived here. He'd stroll along the manicured sidewalk and point out the palaces, marveling at their beauty, telling of trysts with some of the occupants. There's a bond between artists and whores, a dreadful understanding of society. Morgan lived his life with the gusto of a true romantic. He'd done it all. Sex was his canvas.

We continued walking to the top to reach the beautiful vista of the Golden Gate Bridge and the Palace of Fine Arts, the latter a colossal Roman temple, circa 1915, all edged with eucalyptus and cedar trees. Resting a moment at the summit, we breathed in time to noon bell chimes.

"I love you," I said, as my heart found its way to my throat.

"I love you too," Morgan said. But he never looked at me when he said this.

"Sometimes, I think you're afraid of me," I said, my own deep secret tumbling forth. "We say we love each other, but we never do anything about it."

"Our relationship is platonic," Morgan said in defense, panic entering his voice.

"I know, but my feelings are different." I struggled to be honest.

"Well, that's sweet, Gilbert. But no, it's too late for any of that." Morgan looked far away, wistfully, as though his days as a lover were gone, a memory to savor. "Whatever happens, don't stop loving me just because we never had sex."

"Why is it that I always fall for guys who want platonic relationships? Am I ugly or something?"

"No, you're taking it the wrong way. It's not about you; you're great. It's just that I don't have those kinds of feelings for you." Morgan was uncomfortable.

"Maybe the reason I'm addicted to drag and being fabulous is because then I'm desired, at least as an object," I thought aloud. "Of course, it doesn't hurt that all the most gorgeous men flirt attention on me, but when I'm not onstage, it's like I'm not there. My sex life gets channeled into making art. But my valentines only seem to attract impossible unrequited love. Yours, for instance."

"People love your art, but not you? Come on, don't pretend to make your career an altar to sacrifice your heart on or justify your vanity. That's small town. You love the attention. That's what you're really addicted to."

"Vain, *moi*?" I responded in an imitation of Miss Piggy, the Muppet character Morgan said was most representative of the '80s. It made him laugh. He was right; my life was ridiculous. My biggest worry was what I would wear to the next party.

Soon after that walk, Morgan was admitted to Kaiser Hospital. On a cold, rainy spring day, my friend Janice Strassheim picked me up and we drove over. Janice was an angel to Morgan; she visited him every day.

Morgan was in Intensive Care. A nurse made Janice and me put on scrubs and gloves before she directed us to his room with a big red sticker on the door, warning us of the risk of contamination. "Three minutes" was all she said.

Morgan was so glad to see us. He loved the flowers. But, he asked, did we bring him a joint? I sat on his bed, where he was tucked under light blue blankets, and held his hand. Our fingers danced, entwined together. When I finally looked into his eyes, the truth hit me like a freight train: Morgan was dying. I forced a smile and chatted him up about the latest gossip as tears fell from my eyes. It was just water leaking, I sniffed scientifically, to keep my emotions under control. The nurse came in and said we had to leave. Morgan cried when we kissed good-bye. I wondered if it was for the last time.

As Janice piloted her VW back to my house, I broke down into sobs. She tried to comfort me but was crying herself. She told me how much Morgan loved me. It struck me that now, like during another key moment in my life, with Faerie and the birth of the Rainbow Flag, a woman was present to help me along. This time, she was helping me face the death of my best friend. Were it not for dykes like Janice, I would have never survived the AIDS years.

11

Working for the Enemy

One day, on a whim, I asked Jim Ferrigan from Paramount Flag about designing Mayor Feinstein's impending inauguration. Feinstein had been chosen to be mayor by the Board of Supervisors after the Moscone and Milk assassinations in 1978 and was elected to her first full term in 1979 by a slim margin. In November 1983, she was reelected in a landslide. This was to be Dianne Feinstein's coronation.

I showed Jim a sketch I had done of the rotunda of city hall. Impressed, he gave me the phone number of Charlotte Mailliard, rogue queen of San Francisco blue-chip society. She was Feinstein's best friend. Drag queens gossiped that Charlotte picked out Dianne's wardrobe every morning in her Pacific Heights mansion. I rang her up and sent over the drawing.

Unbelievably, I was invited to come in for a meeting to discuss the flags and decor for the event.

Feinstein was the ruling class and had a downtown vision, but there was something real behind the pancake makeup. She loved San Francisco and all of its people—if not the Sisters of Perpetual Indulgence. She had taken flak from both sides as she danced around the issue of gay rights. But I supported her, because she was a Democrat and I hoped she would get behind our struggle. If what Bobbi Campbell was saying about GRID worsening was true, we would need her in the trenches.

I brought sketches over to Charlotte at city hall. She was producing the entire ceremony, as the newly appointed deputy chief of protocol for the city. Charlotte was middle-aged-plus, but attractive and obviously very rich. No face-lift and all business. She reviewed my plan and was impressed. She sent me away with a kiss—and a commission.

Over the next few days, I hung up hundreds of gold-and-white flags in the rotunda of city hall. By using invisible wire, I made them appear suspended in thin air. I also devised an elaborate trick by which, six stories above the marble floor, a huge American flag was rigged to fall out of exploding fireworks. On the night of the inauguration, as a band played "The Stars and Stripes Forever," the flag effect came off perfectly. Thousands of balloons were released from the upper balcony as the American flag floated down from the gilded dome. There were tears in the eyes of people caught up in the rapture of patriotism.

The mayor liked my work. Immediately thereafter I was commissioned to design a state reception for Chinese premier Zhao Ziyang. We were just coming off the Christmas season, and I utilized the red banner of the revolution with five gold stars affixed everywhere, like garlands. After that, I was hired to create fabulous French *drapeaux* and American flags for a visit by President François Mitterrand of France.

Occasionally, I felt like a dilettante artist, working for the enemy. It was both frightening and tempting to think of turning my aesthetic in a more conventional and lucrative direction.

The previous year, San Francisco's Moscone Center had been selected to host the 1984 Democratic National Convention, thanks to strenuous lobbying by Feinstein. I wanted to be a part of it. I was eager to create something incredibly beautiful and purposefully mainstream. The convention became my obsession. I asked Mick Hicks, my friend and a professional photographer, to take photos of the Moscone Center. For the entire winter of 1983, I worked from the photos, carefully constructing illustrations of what my installation would look like.

The first day the convention opened an office in San Francisco, I walked in with a portfolio of designs. I wore a suit and tie, my hair cut short. I was on a mission. I wanted to prove to myself that I could do it. I wanted to work on something more important than the Sisters. I wanted people to take me seriously as an artist. Most of all, I wanted Ken Hughes to love and respect me. Ken liked my drawings; he said that my work was the best he had ever seen.

At the end of May 1984, I finally got a call from the Democratic National Committee, summoning me to the Moscone Center to discuss my proposed flag displays. Bingo! For months on end I'd jumped through countless hoops, drawing endless renderings of my vision for the convention. Until then, they hadn't paid me a dime for any of the sketches nor committed to anything.

After my call with the big money woman, I ran down to the flag factory and announced the good news. However, Ken dampened my enthusiasm; he was convinced that the whole operation, from presidential candidate Walter Mondale on down, were just a bunch of turkeys. Ken's staff agreed with him. The event was only a few weeks away and there were stories in the press about what a mess it was. Still, Jim Ferrigan gave me a lift over to the Democratic headquarters on Howard Street, where I met the convention director and assistant. The director got to the point quickly. "I want the banners to be wispy, like that thing you do with wires sewn in the flags. How much?" I paused; I knew that these were Democrats, not deep-pocketed Republicans. I quoted $14,000 for the first four pieces. The assistant wrote out a check on the spot.

Over the next few weeks, convention reps placed more banner orders with me. I kept working, backed by Paramount. I guided the project from the ink on the first renderings to the complicated cloth constructions, and finally to the structural contours of what I finally came to realize was a flag sculpture. I'd spent eighteen-hour days for weeks making the convention decorations. On the day we shipped it out from Paramount, everyone was so proud. It was total class; even the dozens of large boxes were wrapped in special stars-and-stripes bunting.

Then I had to install every inch of it on-site myself, which took another grueling week. One night at the convention hall, my energy was sapped. When the Secret Service wasn't watching, I slipped into a phone booth near the elevators and snorted cocaine. I never liked coke, but figured it was better than speed, which was killing people right and left.

Morgan had recovered enough to be released from the hospital and sent home to recuperate. We spoke that night. He wanted all the details of the installation—as well as gossip about how Mondale didn't have a prayer. Morgan was voting for Reagan again.

My work on the convention designs continued. Typical of me, I blew the entire budget. I even hired Mick Hicks to take pictures of the project. I organized a portfolio full of his eleven-by-fourteen-inch color glossies. It was worth the thousands I spent on it; that black-ringed book would get me flag jobs for years to come.

The day after the Democratic National Convention ended, I called Morgan. It had been a while, since work had completely overwhelmed me. A recording said the number had been disconnected. I knew what that meant: his parents had blown into town, boxed up all his possessions, and left without ever telling anyone Morgan had died.

I found myself working on an irregular basis, doing more society parties and civic bashes. But I was always known as the guy who made the gay flag—always a little overdressed and too flamboyant to ever really fit into the Bay Area blue-blood scene. Complicating that was the Sisters of Perpetual Indulgence thing. My fate was sealed; I never crossed over the velvet rope. However, I was the gay Betsy Ross and, as Cleve Jones often joked, "a legend in my own mind."

Cleve had graduated from being a member of Harvey Milk's team to his heir apparent. His own legend had been secured with the 1982 publication of Randy Shilts's book *The Mayor of Castro Street*. But Randy got a lot of grief over his book. People howled over his inaccuracies and mythmaking. When I asked him about that, he responded, "They can say it's not accurate, but in two years it will be the truth. Once it's down on paper, it becomes history." I was impressed and a little awed by his defense of artistic license. Randy Shilts wasn't just some chronicler of the movement, he was a storyteller of nonfiction masterpieces.

When Bobbi Campbell passed away on August 15, 1984, I headed into a depression so deep I often slept twelve hours a night. Everything seemed so meaningless. But then Cleve would call me about another political protest and enlist my help. So I'd be sewing and painting banners at a moment's notice. I lived to be angry. And when we'd all march down Market Street, I felt good—Betsy Ross waving the flag.

I harbored immense guilt for not having been there for Morgan at the end. I had believed that the Democratic Convention was more important—that our friendship could wait until I grabbed the brass ring. This alone should have made me reexamine the priorities in my life. But instead, I channeled all my inner rage into more and more art. Sometimes very bad art. Messy paintings, grandiose drawings, trashy scripts for the Sisters. My Singer 107 was churning out ever more outrageous costumes, banners, and variations on the Rainbow Flag.

San Francisco became a ghost town. I'd walk down Castro Street and see bony men shuffling on canes. These were faces that had been healthy and beautiful a few months before. I walked on by, convincing myself that I was not doomed, looking at death with a survivor's indifference. AIDS wasn't happening to me. But half my friends were dead.

In 1985, Cleve came up with another powerful idea. He said that we should put the names of our departed loved ones on pieces of poster board, march them down to the Federal Building, and plaster them all over the damn walls. A group gathered to make them up in my living room. Bill Paul taught us his Magic Marker calligraphy technique, and the pieces began stacking up by the hundreds.

On the morning of our action, Cleve arranged for tall extension ladders to be hidden in the shrubbery around the government office building. When we marched there that evening, thousands of people stormed up the sides and duct-taped these paper tombstones on the edifice. Cleve was already in trouble for the riot after Dan White got off for murdering Harvey, and now he was staging Bastille Day for AIDS. This protest pushed a lot of buttons—and garnered a lot of publicity.

Not long after, Cleve was ready to do it again on a much bigger scale. He had a knack for fixating on the impossible and then demanding the same from everyone. But he wasn't an artist. He could hardly work a staple gun, let alone make any of the props needed for his protests. So he would assemble a team to transform his ideas into visual spectacles. For his latest scheme, there wasn't a name at first. He wanted to transform the Federal Building poster board tombstones into fabric pieces, because they could be so much larger, approaching the scale of the works of Christo, who had wrapped whole islands in fabric. Washington, DC, was Cleve's targeted destination for this happening.

We were in Dennis Peron's kitchen on Seventeenth Street. Dennis was not only San Francisco's leading advocate for legalizing marijuana, he was also an early advocate for the medicinal use of pot for AIDS patients. Cleve was cooking a big spaghetti dinner. I was sitting at the table, yellow legal pad and Bic pen in hand. I was sketching out ways to make Cleve's concept physical, figuring up all the relevant math. How much it would weigh? How many people would it take to put it together? Would the panels be on poles? Or lie on the ground like graves? Or was that desecration? I thought about legalities. What if we didn't get a permit and had to do it covertly? How long would it take to finish the task before we got arrested?

Snap! Snap! Whenever I got bogged down in details, Cleve's fingers were popping in my face. "Forget about that," he would say. "We'll figure it out later."

We were in my sewing room in my new apartment—I'd left the Brain Trust—when Cleve demanded that I make a panel right then—for a political meeting at seven thirty. He held up a sheet he'd just spray-painted with Marvin Feldman's name and it was hideous. Like I said, Cleve wasn't an artist. So for Bobbi Campbell's panel, I hot-glued his name in purple glitz on a three-by-six-foot piece of Day-Glo hot-pink bridal satin left over from a Sisters event. Cleve still wasn't satisfied.

Couldn't I sew it and make it more gorgeous? "Well," I shot back, "do you want it now, or do you want it good?" Our bitchy banter was as legendary as our creative collaborations.

I could tell that Cleve was on to something with these panels. I also knew because he took every opportunity to inform me that this would be his pièce de résistance—his Rainbow Flag, but bigger! Better! "Just move over, bitch," Cleve would tease me. "Your Betsy Ross thing is tired."

Later that day, Cleve and I were at the Women's Building community center, holding up Marvin Feldman's and Bobbi Campbell's panels. The big gay Democratic political club was giving us the once-over. I kept quiet while Cleve explained the whole thing, how everyone should go home and make their own panels for this proposed memorial quilt. Their eyes glazed over with contempt; to them, we were everything that was extreme about the movement. But Cleve Jones is a truly great man, and he needled his way through their armor with the biggest Machiavellian guilt trip anyone had ever seen.

So I was now part of another Cleve project. And working with Cleve became, as always, working *for* Cleve. It meant a kind of love-hate relationship. Cleve turned to others as well, mining their creativity. In the end, all of us, even I, became willing coconspirators in this latest scheme, which would ultimately be known around the world as the NAMES Project AIDS Memorial Quilt.

But our work together was always volatile. One evening, Cleve and I were at Dennis Peron's house, planning yet another event connected to the NAMES Project. Planning led to a disagreement, and then a disagreement led to a spat between two men with very large egos. Cleve knew my weakest spots; he would control a situation by making nasty comments, mercilessly pushing my buttons. Suddenly, I stood up, leaned over the kitchen table, and slapped Cleve across the face. He cursed me and left. We didn't speak for two years.

Who owns an idea? Who owns a vision? All this egomania between Cleve and me brought up my own insecurities about James and Faerie and their roles as collaborators in the creation of the Rainbow Flag. As

James and Faerie were to me, I became to Cleve: the witness to the miracle.

I accepted the mythology Cleve spun around the genesis of the quilt, that he was the sole creator, that it really was his baby. Ideas are the property of those who make them realities. I came to appreciate the deeper ironies about authorship and shrugged off the inevitable comparisons between ownership of the flag and ownership of the quilt. After all, we weren't the first to make spectacular environmental art out of fabric; Christo was the king. He had sewn up celebrity and fine art long ago. Cleve and I watched him scale the heights, knowing that Christo's level of global fame was not available to a couple of big queers from San Francisco.

12

Stoning the Pope

E very day I read several newspapers, front to back. One morning, I spotted a filler piece, about two inches long, announcing that Pope John Paul II would be coming to the United States in the fall of 1987. I was furious, but I thought that if the pope came to San Francisco, it would be a perfect opportunity to protest the Catholic Church's anti-gay oppression.

There was nothing in the papers about what cities the pope was to visit, so I went to the mayor's protocol office undercover to sniff out information. I looked sharp in my butch attire of crisp red polo shirt, black slacks, and shiny red shoes. I visited under the pretense that I was vying for a job to create displays for the fiftieth anniversary of the Golden Gate Bridge, even bringing some design sketches. By this time, I'd made countless drawings for parties I had decorated. "Everybody, look what Gilbert brought!" the office ladies squealed.

The various aides gathered round and enthused over the fabulously detailed, jumbo-size sketches. The ladies were all smiles. I played it cool, casually asking if the pope was scheduled to visit. I told them I had some ideas for welcoming banners. One secretary told me the unofficial date was September 18, 1987, but details were still in the works. I thanked her and left to poke around city hall for more clues. I learned that His Holiness would be setting up his tent right in Mission Dolores, a church right in the middle of the world's largest gay community. I headed home to start planning the offensive.

The date of the papal visit grew closer, and my determination to make a stand against the Church's oppression only grew. When his itinerary was officially confirmed, I found it ironic that the pope would arrive in San Francisco on the two hundredth anniversary of the signing of the US Constitution. Church and state would collide right on our front porch! What's more, in October 1986, the Vatican released its latest guidance on pastoral care, a letter by the Congregation for the Doctrine of the Faith. It declared homosexuality "an intrinsic moral evil." The Vatican's ongoing homophobia basically sanctioned violence against lesbians and gays.

By early 1987, I had recruited Sister Sadie the Jewish nun to help me. My idea was to turn the pope's visit into not a rock show but a rock throw! The big guy's motorcade through Holland a few years earlier had been met by angry gay mobs who targeted the white Popemobile with rocks and bottles. The Dutch were on the right track.

Sadie and I returned to city hall to register as "the Official 1987 San Francisco Papal Welcoming Committee." By laying claim to these words, we screwed up the Vatican's merchandising possibilities. And in a mocking flash of art we created "Papal Bonds" with gold seals, issued by me and Sister Sadie to raise money for our protest.

But first came the Golden Gate Bridge anniversary. I didn't end up working on it, but that didn't stop me from showing up at the event. I came as a drag parody of Bay Area social ladies, dressed in a gold sequined power suit and calling myself Charlotte Mylar. The party, put together by these Marie Antoinettes, turned into a massive gridlock of celebrants that caused the middle of the bridge to dip seven feet.

When the pope finally toured San Francisco four months later, events took an unexpected turn. At six o'clock in the morning on the day of his arrival, someone knocked on my door. When I opened up, a stack of papers was shoved into my fumbling fingers. Sadie and I were being sued in US district court for trademark infringement by the Sisters of Perpetual Indulgence Inc.

Papal Bond issued by Sister Chanel 2001 and Sister Sadie, signed by the Reverend Mother. *Created by Gilbert Baker, from the collection of Mark Rennie*

It was all over postcards and a pie. The first infraction? Sadie and I had been hired a few months earlier to pose in nun garb for a line of postcards. What irritated the other sisters was that the photographer only wanted the two of us. We got a total of $600 for the job.

Then there was the incident involving Sister Boom Boom, a.k.a. Jack Fertig. Jack was the reigning diva of the Sisters. We never liked each other, acting like Crawford and Davis adversaries, competing for laughs in the backstage makeup mirror and pushing each other out of the footlights. Boom Boom was always emcee at events, but she never prepared, just showing up at the last minute. And often she would bomb. I had decided to do something about it.

Every couple of years, the Sisters would organize a charity basketball game. The most recent one involved two all-lesbians teams, and the bleachers were filled with screaming lesbian fans. I was to be named Game Queen after the game in a special ceremony. It was going to be fabulous. Twenty people would be dressed in cardinal-red Bemberg silk that I had created for the elaborate coronation. I even made them little cardinal hats. It all screamed Vatican pomp. Except I was the only one in sequins.

That night, I ran onto the basketball floor to Spanish disco music and the crowd began screaming. Then I turned a perfect cartwheel in my high stilettos and low-cut, floor-length, Halston-inspired gown. Then I sashayed back up to center court, where I knelt on a red velvet pillow, prepared to be named Game Queen.

Sadie read a proclamation and I was crowned—not with the usual beauty pageant tiara but with a pope-style miter, made out of the American flag and glittering with jewels. Four thousand ticket holders cheered loudly, drowning out the National Anthem being played by the gay band. Then I stood and waved in my best Brian De Palma *Carrie* pose, holding a huge bouquet of roses, five feet wide.

The lights came up, and Sister Boom Boom arrived right on cue to get the microphone. That's when I did it. Locating the box hidden in the bouquet, I slid my fingers under a cream pie. Gracefully, I shoved it right smack into Boom Boom's face. The crowd fell into stunned silence and then slowly began laughing, thinking this was part of the routine—not noticing the horror on the faces of the assembled sisters.

I thought I was going to be excommunicated. But the Sisters ended up suing me instead. SISTERS SPLIT was the front-page headline in the gay rags.

Everybody abandoned me that day of the pope's visit, not wanting any of the lawsuit shit to get on them. So all my protest ideas—gays throwing rocks at the Popemobile—went right down the drain.

Still, I had a backup plan. While the pope's helicopter was arriving, Sadie and I and a couple of others crashed a car into the tollgate of the Golden Gate Bridge. We were arrested on the spot. When the police tried to put the handcuffs on, they spread my arms wide. Attached to my wrists were the corners of the US Constitution in parchment satin that opened across my bosom. The media caught the moment. It was better than giving John Paul II the finger.

They took our mug shots in full drag at the Hall of Justice. We were fingerprinted, given a ticket, and released in time to go home and watch the motorcade on live TV.

In the end, San Francisco stayed home when the pope rolled into town. It was one big snub. Less than twenty-five thousand lined the streets. Only two thousand showed up for the official protest. Overall, it was one big snub. The Popemobile passed empty blocks, the pontiff waving to an invisible crowd.

Just a few weeks later, another visiting dignitary was greeted by a party I'd designed for the mayor's office. It was a reception for Juan Carlos, the king of Spain, at the Palace of the Legion of Honor overlooking the Golden Gate Bridge. I turned flags into secular crosses, and the king himself thanked me with a hug.

After word of my pope protest spread, however, Mayor Feinstein's office never hired me again.

Lawyers later convened an arbitration meeting between Sadie and me and the Sisters. The plaintiffs laid out a list of demands and dictated what Sadie and I could wear and not wear from now on. They forbade the use of whiteface, claiming it was their "intellectual property."

"Well," I said, "If they have a problem with that, they should talk to Ringling Brothers."

13

Rock Bottom
and Rebel Rebirth

It wasn't long before I found myself a dinosaur, a forgotten relic. I was shunned not just by downtown but by the greater gay community—both the respectable ones making quilt panels and the brash ones ACT-ing UP. I was broke and depressed beyond all hope. There was nowhere to go but down. One day, I found my way to the Golden Gate Bridge and thought about jumping off. As I deliberated, the highway patrol arrived and stopped me. They threw me into a squad car and I was briefly locked up in a psych ward.

After my escapade on the bridge railing, I was embarrassed. It was very hard to talk about my depression. But soon after I got out, Cleve called me, demanding that I pull myself together. He reminded me that there was more work to be done. Our struggle wasn't over. And, Cleve being Cleve, he told me that in spite of all my failures and transgressions, he was still my friend.

So I returned to working with Tom Taylor at his new workshop on Isis Street, sewing whatever small jobs I could find. My time with the Sisters of Perpetual Indulgence was over. But a new muse came into my life. Carol Leigh was a sex worker activist who called herself Scarlot Harlot. While creating outrageous outfits for Scarlot, I was inspired to reinvent myself with a new street theater persona. Betsy Ross debuted at the Haight Ashbury Street Fair, dressed in outrageous flag drag, accompanied by Scarlot and Sadie. When we showed off our stars-and-stripes gowns, it was like wearing fireworks. People only saw us as a whore and a couple of drag queens ridiculing the American flag. Some drunk redneck hippies even threw beer cans at us, but the police rescued us from the mob. It was exciting, provoking that kind of reaction.

I now had a new identity: Betsy Ross, flag desecrator. I loved that—it summed up the extremes in my life. But it was a complete put-on, as nobody loved the American flag as much as I did. Sure, I was always the first to light a match—but never to desecrate and always to instigate.

People called it desecration, but they didn't know what that really meant legally. Cutting up and even burning the American flag were acts protected as free speech under the Constitution. We had every right as artists to express ourselves using this sacred symbol. The hippies wore jeans made out of flags. *Hustler* publisher Larry Flynt wore it as a diaper in federal court. Protesters burned it on the streets of foreign capitals and in front of government buildings right here at home. Wearing the actual flag was a statement about freedom; it announced you as a radical, a revolutionary.

Dressing up to blow people's minds was better than being a movie star, because the streets were better than the screen for scaring the shit out of everyone. The real connection to the public happens with confrontation at the boundaries of fear. Art is like a gun that way.

The shooting of sacred cows began in earnest.

14

Pink Jesus and the Holy War

In 1990, I crashed the San Francisco Lesbian and Gay Freedom Day Parade. I did it dressed as Jesus Christ, covered head to toe in pink.

"Pink Jesus" was a protest of many things I was pissed off about. I was protesting Senator Jesse Helms, the North Carolina homophobe trying to kill the National Endowment for the Arts because of its support of gay art. Our First Amendment rights were under fire. I was also fed up with the Freedom Day organizers, who controlled every aspect of the event. They had grown more conservative, asking drag and leather marchers to cool it. More censorship.

Senator Helms was running for reelection in November, and recently the Miller Brewing Company had been exposed for contributing money to his campaign. The news sparked boycotts of Miller beer in gay bars across America. But the parade bigwigs had decided to ignore the national protest and accept $30,000 in Miller sponsorship money.

Pink Jesus was born in Tom Taylor's workshop. Fred Herzog and Jerry Schreyer painted my entire body fluorescent pink, using sponges to daub on water-based theatrical makeup. I had crafted a crown of thorns to offset pink heels and a burnt American flag as my loincloth. Completing the spectacle was a big wooden cross, also bright pink. Fred and Jerry sprayed a fixative all over my skin that froze every goose bump in place.

Tom loaded all of us and my cross pieces into the back of his pickup and we drove downtown. I had to sit on a plastic sheet because the body paint smudged easily, even lacquered over. We double-parked at the corner of Spear and Mission Streets and ran the short block up to Market Street, where the Freedom Day Parade was about to kick off. Adrenaline pulsed head to toe.

The last few motorcycles from the Dykes on Bikes contingent had just sped off. The official parade committee was lined up behind their banner, preparing, as tradition dictated, to lead the procession.

Not this year.

I clicked my pink high heels three times, adjusted my American flag loincloth, and crashed the front of the parade. Fred quickly assembled the cross, which included big nails to clench in my hands so I could pose crucified. On top of the assemblage was a chartreuse note proclaiming, MARTYRS FOR ART, an homage to late photographer Robert Mapplethorpe, a primary, posthumous target of Helms's NEA attack.

Fred and Jerry unfurled my banner, which read, NOT SPONSORED BY JESSE HELMS. It stretched out, curb to curb, seventy-five feet wide. I could hear gasps of outrage. This was a direct slam of the parade committee, which had hung a gigantic Miller beer advertisement over the main stage. As I marched closer to the media area, a member of the parade's board of directors suddenly grabbed my fluorescent pink arm. "You're ruining everything!" she screeched. "You have no right to be here!" Into her walkie-talkie, she barked for security. But she was swept aside by a crush of photographers intent on capturing the blasphemous image of Pink Jesus. When security arrived, they couldn't get through the throngs of news cameras to reach me.

"Arrest him!" one of the security people told the police.

"For what," I spat back. "A fashion violation?"

The crowd roared at such absurdity. The police weren't about to touch anything as harmless as Pink Jesus. Parade organizers, outdone and unglued, retreated behind their teensy banner and pretended I didn't exist. They marched a hundred yards behind the biblical spectacle for the duration of the parade.

Pink Jesus was covered in all the newspapers and magazines. I wondered how many zillion gallons of special pink ink had to be mixed to print so many pictures. As a political cartoon, the crucifixion of Jesus by a drag queen was outrageous—a burned American flag covering my private parts. Was it desecration? Was it unpatriotic? Did it go too far? Christian fundamentalists had a field day. Churches sent out images of me in pink makeup to their faithful donors, demanding donations to stop blasphemy in San Francisco. Pink Jesus raked in millions for them.

And then Pink Jesus set off a holy war. A TV preacher called the faithful together to stop Satan, exhorting them to attend an evangelical gathering in San Francisco, a.k.a. Sin Central, on Halloween of that year. Congregations of every stripe headed to the San Francisco Civic Auditorium in buses, calling themselves "prayer warriors."

I decided that Pink Jesus deserved an encore. Dressed in my fluorescent makeup, I led a huge group of Halloween celebrators to the Civic Auditorium. I demanded entrance to see the producer of the show. Behind me, ten thousand people pushed against police barricades, dressed in every conceivable costume. The prayer warriors cowered inside—and it was captured on live TV.

I received more press coverage for Pink Jesus, but I also drew more critics. If they didn't want to kill me, people thought me a fool. I learned that pink is very dangerous, and I washed off the paint for the last time. Years afterward, Cleve would bring up Pink Jesus whenever anyone took me too seriously. He teased me about the episode to remind me that his image-making skills were superior to mine.

It was now the spring of 1991, and we had seen a decade of AIDS already. Everyone was living with it, even if they weren't HIV positive. Death, pain, suffering, and anguish were day-to-day reality in gay San Francisco.

During the '80s, AIDS agencies had sprung up everywhere. Benefit dinners and grants from sponsors. Confused theories and crackpot cures.

Charlatans and angels. People took off their Doc Martens combat boots and put on tuxedos with red ribbons. Out of the streets and into rented ballrooms. We street activists hated it.

The morbid glamour of the immense holocaust was beginning to wear off. What more could be said? Cleve Jones had created the NAMES Project AIDS Memorial Quilt years ago. It apparently wasn't enough. And now Cleve was diagnosed. He officially had it.

Cleve had only contempt for the state of gay affairs and shouted to the highest heavens in righteous protest. And now, thanks to the AIDS Quilt, he had a national forum for his anger. TV's *60 Minutes* covered him. Magazines wrote about him. ABC News named him Person of the Week. Cleve was one of the most famous homosexuals alive. He was also brilliant beyond all madness, with a new idea every minute.

The idea for Pink Saturday was born on a hike up the steep cliffs of Red Rock Hill. It was one of Cleve's favorite places. There, we looked out over the city, and the Castro was a toy village at our feet. Cleve, in an expansive mood, scrambled up to the very tip-top boulder. There, on the wind-chiseled precipice, he raised his arms up like Moses and relayed to the assembled mortals his latest vision: a big street party to be held in the Castro the night before the annual Freedom Day Parade. Hundreds of thousands of people would pay admission, with proceeds benefiting community service organizations.

And just like that, I was on board, working with Cleve—again.

Why not? I was tired of the efforts to make the Rainbow Flag a part of the annual parade. I had kissed a lot of ass and eaten a lot of condescending bullshit to get anything to happen with the flag. After a decade of hassling with stupid and corrupt parade organizers, I felt helpless against the consensus of mediocrity stifling my artistic expression. I wanted a blank canvas, something new. The parade was twenty years old and needed new energy. Pink Saturday was an opportunity to create something fabulous. A new gay holiday was born.

Cleve loved colored smoke and bursting bombs, so he looked into a way to get fireworks to explode over Castro and Market Streets at the climax of the event. We could set off rockets from the top of Red Rock Hill, timed to music by Pink Floyd.

A permit was issued and I took charge. I mapped out the whole extravaganza in detail and then created a storyboard for the vast production, including mirrored balls, dancing multitudes, and dazzling special effects. Art Agnos was now mayor and he supported it; he reasoned that the city would make a fortune from tourists attending Pink Saturday.

Cleve's role was to be the producer. But, as usual, he balked at doing any real work and brought in Joe van Es–Ballesteros from the NAMES Project and City Supervisor Roberta Achtenberg's office to help run things. Cleve was always in charge, sort of. But when the going got tough, Cleve got invisible. Luckily, Joe was a spitfire of organizational skills. He knew everybody. He set up his Rolodex in an office overlooking Castro and Eighteenth Streets. The two of us would put it all together. "You're the director," he reminded me one day, "but don't forget that you answer to me, because I have to deal with Cleve."

The parade committee was still locked in its torrid love affair with the Miller Brewing Company. So I called up Budweiser to sponsor Pink Saturday. The party was on. Allen White, the veteran local publicist, joined in. The two of us drove down to King City in a rented rig to pick up pallets stacked with a hundred thousand pink souvenir programs. A true production wizard, Allen thought big; he got all the area lesbian and gay marching bands to form a twilight parade. The hot new dance combo Voice Farm agreed to headline. A sound system and lasers would transform Market Street into an open-air disco.

But as soon as we began working, soap opera and political intrigue intervened. The old guard was intent on chopping down this brash, upstart activism. Jealous tongues wagged; knives were out. City hall was deluged with calls trying to stop us. I spent long afternoons in diners commiserating with my friend, feminist and author Phyllis Burke. Over coffee and meat loaf, milk shakes and cherry pie, I shared my growing cynicism. "It's like black magic, dark forces tainting Pink Saturday."

Phyllis agreed. "Of course they're out to get you and Cleve. If artists can organize a better gay pride celebration, then what use is there for a parade committee? Ability and imagination are the enemy of incompetent bureaucrats. As artists, you should stay true to your vision."

That was easy to say, but every day we faced another compromise to our plans, another smear campaign to fend off. Attempts were made to pull our permits just a few days before the event. But Joe handled it all.

That Saturday morning, cumulus clouds hung low in the sky, the exact shades of a Maxfield Parrish painting. It rained, and the streets were clean. At 5:00 PM, two hours ahead of our permit, a quarter-million people filled the neighborhood, ready to party. They were dazed by the sound systems, the galactic light show, the sheer fabulosity of it. The afternoon was so hot, many took off their clothes and danced in their underwear.

But in the end, Pink Saturday was a disaster. We spent about $90,000 and only took in $80,000. Cleve ended up paying the debt, for which I was mostly responsible. When news of our financial fiasco came to light, the chill began to set in. Community service organizations that expected to benefit from the event began sniping. Forget that none of these groups had invested money or mobilized volunteers as asked. They all placed the blame on Cleve, Joe, and me. The situation was made worse when Cleve suddenly flew off to Spain as the controversy exploded. People began asking me with a straight face if Cleve had a secret Swiss bank account and a château in the south of France.

The failure of Pink Saturday hounded Cleve. When he decided to run for the San Francisco Board of Supervisors in 1992, Pink Saturday was one of the issues that detractors brought up. It was a black mark on his record of community service. Gay newspapers withheld their endorsement.

Election night that November was a twister of jubilation that tore through the streets of the Castro. George Bush was out. We sang, "Ding Dong! The Witch Is Dead." Arkansas's Bill Clinton got elected president with one of the lowest popular vote percentages ever. Spin doctors said lesbian and gay support had done it for him. Supervisor Roberta Achtenberg called from Clinton's Little Rock headquarters and we patched her into the public address system.

But it wasn't a victorious night for Cleve. The gay establishment had hung Cleve out to dry. He was defeated. The loss was so humiliating, he dropped out of the city scene and moved north to the Russian River and focused on his fragile health. He had recently acquired Pneumocystis pneumonia and was now allergic to the drug prescribed to treat it.

In the end, Cleve turned out to be the real Pink Jesus. San Francisco had initially worshipped his every achievement, and then crucified him for one failure. He never let me forget about Pink Saturday. "It's all your fault" he joked. But in my heart, I knew he wasn't kidding.

Cleve traveled the world, but I never left California. "This town is too small for you," he warned. "Get out before you get stuck." He urged me to go to the March on Washington for Lesbian, Gay and Bi Equal Rights and Liberation in April 1993. But I couldn't afford to travel to DC. Besides, it just seemed like another march to me. At the last moment, everybody else jetted off to be there. Tumbleweed blew here where cable cars roamed. More than one million people converged on the capital in the largest lesbian and gay event in American history. I watched the C-SPAN coverage alone in my living room.

As thousands of people waved Rainbow Flags in front of famous monuments, it appeared like an immense sea of color. I suddenly was stirred with an idea: I wanted to do something for the twenty-fifth anniversary of the Stonewall riots in New York City in June 1994.

When Cleve came home from the DC march, he offered to help. We began planning at his cottage on the banks of the Russian River. At night, we would take long walks under the towering redwoods and shoot ideas back and forth about what we might contribute to the Stonewall anniversary. "Anything to get you out of here," he quipped. "You've already ruined my life."

Cleve was always a size queen. His AIDS Memorial Quilt covered acres. "You should do something with the Rainbow Flag—a really big one," he said. "Something incredible."

The vision came: I decided to make something even bigger than the quilt: the world's longest flag.

Christmas 1955. As an artistic child, Gilbert felt trapped by conservative Kansas life. *Courtesy of Patricia Baker*

LEFT: Easter 1965. Gilbert and his father in their Wichita home. As Gilbert took an interest in America's counterculture, the rift between father and son widened. RIGHT: In 1972, Gilbert was discharged from the army and embraced a new life in San Francisco. *Courtesy of Patricia Baker*

Gilbert in San Francisco in the late 1970s. *Photo by Mark Rennie*

Gilbert's silk screen poster for the 1978 Gay Freedom Day Parade. *Photo by Mark Rennie*

Before running the original Rainbow Flags up the flagpole, Gilbert and Walter Caplan (far left) tested the rigging for durability on June 23, 1978. At right, local street performer Jim Kerley. *Photo by Mark Rennie*

Birth of an icon. Gilbert and volunteers raise the original Rainbow Flags over San Francisco's United Nations Plaza on Gay Freedom Day, June 25, 1978. *Photo by James McNamara, from the collection of Mick Hicks*

LEFT: Gilbert in self-designed garb as Miss Liberty. San Francisco, 1980. *Photo by Mick Hicks*

RIGHT: Gilbert, front row, middle nun. In 1981, he became a novice with the Sisters of Perpetual Indulgence, a Bay Area group of street theater activists. *Marie Ueda Collection (2006-12), courtesy of the Gay, Lesbian, Bisexual, Transgender Historical Society*

Gilbert's 1980 watercolor sketch for a plan to decorate San Francisco's city hall. *Photo by Mark Rennie*

Gilbert prepares the rotunda of city hall for Dianne Feinstein's mayoral reelection party in 1983. *Gilbert Baker Estate*

When San Francisco hosted the Democratic National Convention in 1984, Gilbert lobbied successfully to decorate San Francisco's Moscone Center. *Photo by Mick Hicks*

November 27, 1983. Gilbert as a ferocious Lady Justice to commemorate the fifth anniversary of the murders of City Supervisor Harvey Milk and Mayor George Moscone. *Photo by Daniel Nicoletta*

Cleve Jones and Gilbert mark the seventh anniversary of the assassinations of Milk and Moscone in 1985. *Photo by Mick Hicks*

During one Gay Freedom Day parade, Gilbert introduced another of his star-spangled drag alter egos: Betsy Ross. *Photo by Mick Hicks*

Gilbert as Sister Chanel 2001. This postcard infuriated fellow Sisters, resulting in a lawsuit and his expulsion from the group.

Photo by Jim West, West Cards

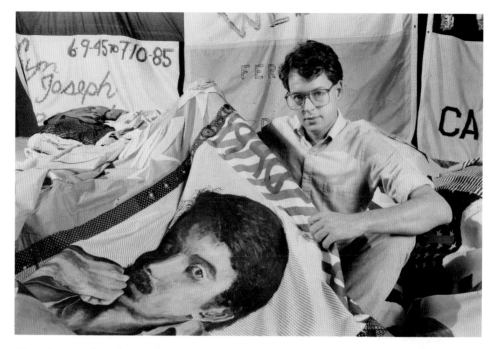

Cleve Jones with early panels from the NAMES Project AIDS Memorial Quilt. *From the collection of Cleve Jones*

Gilbert as Pink Jesus, protesting corporate underwriting of the 1990 San Francisco Lesbian and Gay Freedom Day Parade. The image of Pink Jesus ran in newspapers across the country, igniting religious fundamentalist outrage. *Robert Pruzan Papers (1998-36), courtesy of the Gay, Lesbian, Bisexual, Transgender Historical Society*

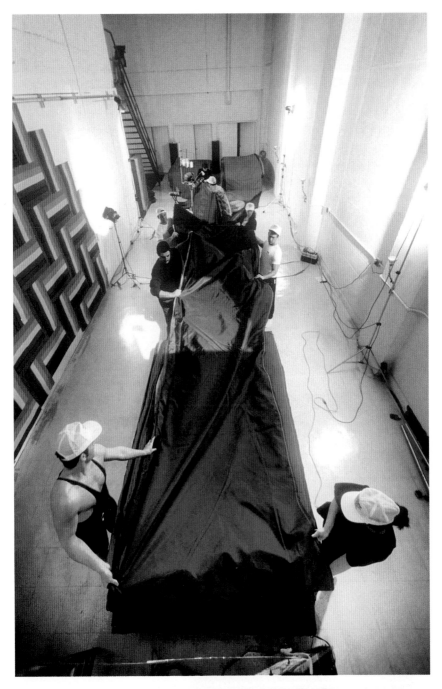

Gilbert's New York City workshop, where he created the mile-long Rainbow Flag for Stonewall 25 in 1994. Volunteers help fold the mammoth banner.

Photo by Mick Hicks

As city politicians battled with gay activists over the Stonewall 25 parade route, Gilbert worked days and nights to complete the flag. *Photo by Mick Hicks*

A momentary truce between Cleve Jones and Gilbert, longtime political comrades who were constantly at odds during the embattled Raise the Rainbow project. *Photo by Mick Hicks*

The first annual Drag March in New York City's East Village on June 24, 1994. Gilbert (center) carries the event banner in one hand and a silver high heel in the other. *Photo by Mick Hicks*

Stonewall 25, the morning of June 26, 1994. Gilbert's friend Tom Taylor unloads the three-and-a-half-ton Rainbow Flag for volunteers to carry along the First Avenue parade route. *Photo by Charley Beal*

Clad in a silver sequined gown, Gilbert dances among the billows of the mile-long Rainbow Flag at Stonewall 25.

Photo by Daniel Nicoletta

Thousands of volunteers worked in unison to carry the mile-long flag on First Avenue. None knew what secret plans Gilbert had for the banner. *Photo by Charley Beal*

Photographer Mick Hicks, shooting from a helicopter, captures the moment (at the bottom of the photo) when Gilbert scissored through the flag for a surprise protest march on Fifth Avenue. *Photo by Mick Hicks*

The guerrilla flag pieces, cut from the mile-long banner, are rejoined on Fifth Avenue for the Stonewall 25 alternative march. *Photo by Mick Hicks*

LEFT: Gilbert and fellow protestors march the Rainbow Flag triumphantly past St. Patrick's Cathedral, the headquarters of New York City's anti-gay Catholic archdiocese. RIGHT: Gilbert found a powerful ally in activist Richard Ferrara, who helped create the mile-long flag. *Photos by Charley Beal*

San Francisco Lesbian, Gay, Bisexual, Transgender Pride Celebration, 1998. Gilbert Baker led the parade to mark the twentieth anniversary of the creation of the Rainbow Flag. *Photo by Daniel Nicoletta*

Cleve Jones (center) pitched in to help Gilbert in Key West, Florida, in 2003. There, the gay Betsy Ross set a new world's record by sewing a 1.25-mile Rainbow Flag that extended from the Atlantic Ocean to the Gulf of Mexico. *Photo by Mick Hicks*

Always a political visionary, Gilbert responded to the 2016 election of President Donald Trump by creating replicas of World War II prisoner uniforms worn by gay men in Nazi death camps.
Gilbert Baker Estate

A career highlight: Gilbert presents a hand-dyed Rainbow Flag to President Obama at the White House's 2016 LGBT Pride Month reception. *Courtesy of the Barack Obama Presidential Library*

Gilbert as Busty Ross, crowned "Most Political" drag queen at the 2012 Invasion of the Pines on Fire Island. *Photo by Charley Beal*

Gilbert's final creation. In March 2017, he sewed a special limited-edition set of nine-color Rainbow Flags to mark the banner's thirty-ninth anniversary. *Photo by Richard Ferrara*

15

Spreading My Wings

Once I had dreamed up the idea to create the world's longest Rainbow Flag, I had to research how to make it a reality. I decided it would be a mile long and carried through the streets of Manhattan for New York City Pride 1994, already renamed Stonewall 25 to commemorate the anniversary of the 1969 Stonewall riots.

I made some sketches, then dialed coast to coast for prices and specs from manufacturers. Cleve thought of ways to sell the project as a fundraiser. His activist work had brought him into corporate boardrooms to raise a mint for the NAMES Project. AIDS had touched the Fortune 500; captains of industry started showing up at benefits, both they and their trophy wives wearing red ribbons.

We would discuss angles at the kitchen table at my new digs, Dennis Peron's house on Eighteenth Street. Cleve would make his ginger chicken and a salad. We'd drink chardonnay and look onto Dennis's starlit flower garden while listening to a Peter Gabriel record of African liberation anthems. Hanging out with Cleve meant listening to sixty ideas a minute. His appetite for life and sticky pleasure was legendary. Clever, brilliant, ambitious, a ruthless intellectual, funny and grand—that's what I admired about Cleve Jones. He didn't make apologies for who he was. He thought only of the future. The NAMES Project had even been the subject of the Academy Award–winning documentary *Common Threads*.

Some in the community were critical of Cleve's fundraising; they questioned the political correctness of selling sponsorships for what was, in essence, a collective funeral for the fallen. But Cleve was undaunted; he racked up frequent flyer miles by traveling around the country, giving speeches and getting plaques. He had just signed on as a consultant to Stadtlanders, a mail-order pharmacy on the East Coast. He was determined to help revolutionize the way people with AIDS got their drugs. He planned to bypass the government red tape and work directly with an independent pharmacy.

At the next big consultation meeting with Stadtlanders, Cleve casually mentioned my idea of creating the mile-long flag. They jumped on it. When he returned home, Cleve gave me the good news, adding in that way he had of joking but not joking, "You'll owe me for the rest of your life."

I was working with Cleve yet again. In *Webster's Dictionary*, *collaboration* is defined in a few different ways: "1. to work jointly with others . . . 2. to cooperate with or willingly assist an enemy . . ."

Friends scoffed. The notion that Cleve and I would team up again defied reason. Pink Saturday had been a catastrophe, and we still bickered over who was responsible. Though we remained friends and drew closer, even rooming together, it was always touch and go. But whenever Cleve and I worked together, we made magic.

Amazingly, Cleve was able to get Stadtlanders to tentatively agree to a grant of $250,000 to build the world's longest flag for Stonewall 25. The figure was unprecedented. One thing was not negotiable, however: Cleve made sure all profits would go to AIDS nutrition and meal programs.

Of course, we wouldn't really be collaborators for the Stonewall 25 project in the true sense. While I held the titles of artist and project creator, I would serve as Cleve's underling as he served the corporate interests. He let me know that I would be expected to defer to him on every matter.

I complained about Cleve's ground rules over coffee with my friend Phyllis Burke. She had recently authored a new book, *Family Values*, a commentary on how new types of families were being formed, especially by nontraditional same-sex couples. She had her opponents, but Phyllis handled talk show and shock radio appearances with cool passion and common sense.

"Compromise is the art of public art," I told her. "Everything I do takes so much human effort that in the end it's not really mine. I guess that's success. The hard part is trading away all the control while holding on to your integrity."

Phyllis wondered aloud whether Cleve and I could work together again. She was skeptical.

I acknowledged the challenges. "Genius requires the faith of Icarus," I told her.

"Then this is your moment, Gilbert," Phyllis said. "Ascend."

My wings were metaphorical. But now I was really flying. At thirty-five thousand feet, to be specific—in a 737 en route to New York City to explore the mechanics of the Stonewall 25 flag project. It was July 1993. I had done my preliminary homework; my briefcase bulged with aerial photographs and maps. Cleve was in the seat next to me. My heart raced as I peered through the window, anticipating my first glimpse of Manhattan.

16

Dorothy Goes to Gotham

Outside the airplane window, New York City emerged through the clouds. I marveled at the reflection of skyscrapers in the glimmering East River. It was a mirage of ziggurats, deep-brown silhouettes throbbing in the golden afternoon. I gazed at the Empire State Building and the Chrysler Building, which looked just like all the postcards I had seen for years.

And I could see all these marvels with a clarity I'd never experienced before. Cleve had convinced me to start wearing glasses, after years of telling me, "You're blind as a bat!"

Cleve led the way through baggage claim. Every breath of city air felt different, as if the oxygen couldn't contain the energy. In the backseat of a yellow cab, we smoked cigarettes with the windows down while Cleve planned the itinerary. After checking in to the trendy Paramount Hotel and finishing off some delicious room service, we went out for a walk—our first scouting mission to ensure we could make the mile-long flag project happen.

We passed Times Square and Rockefeller Center, our tennis shoes gliding over the sidewalks on our way to Fifth Avenue. At St. Patrick's Cathedral, we made a left and headed north toward Central Park. This was where the flag would begin its journey in the Stonewall 25 parade. When the traffic lights changed, Cleve and I ran into the street with a tape measure, calculating just how a mile-long flag would fit on the world's most famous avenue. The two of us went over every detail as we walked under the stars in the urban summer heat.

The design and construction of the Rainbow Flag was my province. Cleve's job was to deal with the sponsors, and recruit and organize the volunteers. We estimated it would take ten thousand of them to unfurl and carry a piece of cloth that would measure 5,280 feet long and 30 feet wide.

In the morning, Cleve was up early to catch another flight. He would return in a couple of days after a speaking engagement. I had the day to myself but a very focused agenda. I headed to the East Village. Destination: 9 Bleecker Street, slightly west of the Bowery. This address was an infamous hotbed of New York radical activity—a long-running commune filled with hippies, anarchists, freaks, pot decriminalization advocates, and AIDS activists.

Alice Torbush had been watching my scheduled approach from upstairs. She opened a broken window on the top floor and waved hello. I was welcomed through the splintered wooden front door and we hugged each other warmly.

Number 9 was a trip back in time to the days of Abbie Hoffman and the Yippies. On every wall hung posters, floor to ceiling, from long-forgotten protest marches, demonstrations, and general rabble-rousing. Dusty rooms smelled of old books, yellowing newsprint, and the piss of a pride of cats. Yippie cofounder Dana Beal had been living there for years, as had Alice, who was the "political commissar" for *Overthrow*, a tabloid devoted to revolution. Since 1979, it had reported on the political situations (and American interventions) in Iran and Nicaragua. I was a devoted fan.

Dana was away on a trip. I followed Alice up the stairs to her turf on the top floor. We smoked a joint, reminiscing about the '70s and gossiping about mutual friends on the West Coast—Cleve and Dennis Peron. Alice was amused that I might be living in New York while I worked on the mile-long Rainbow Flag. She wanted to hear all of the plans. As I shared details, her eyes made little check marks. She was very knowledgeable about organizing on the New York scene.

She warned me of a new contender for mayor. Rudolph Giuliani was part of an emerging trend in which large cities were electing Republican moderates, a backlash against Clinton and the ascending Democrats in Washington. This could have consequences for Stonewall 25.

"Let's put it this way," Alice said. "New York ain't San Francisco. Giuliani is no Frank Jordan. He's got brains. His whole act is dangerous; it's all about the management of minorities. Giuliani is gonna get elected standing up to people like us, stopping us. He's a cop, and cops will rule. If I were you, I'd get a lawyer." She warned that a Mayor Giuliani would have no patience for a massive event like mine—especially a gay one. I replied that bringing in lawyers would scare Cleve and the pharmacy. I had just assumed the Stonewall 25 organizers enjoyed the same civic support in New York as gay activists in San Francisco. As I considered the possibility that the city might be an obstacle, a dark cloud formed.

The television announced that it was 101 degrees in New York City. Number 9 had no air conditioner. Alice led the way to the fire escape, where we took another toke and tried to imagine a breeze.

"Look, here comes Charley," Alice said, pointing to a man roller-blading down the street. I watched him roll around in small, precise circles, graceful and boyishly handsome. Dana had once confided he had a gay younger brother, but Dana was so straight, it seemed impossible genetically. Charley was an art director for mainstream TV and films.

Charley Beal came up to the roof, all bright-eyed, and introduced himself. "You're from San Francisco?" he asked. "I love San Francisco—so many beautiful men and fog." He had brought along some drinks and served them with ice.

Alice explained my background as the creator of the Rainbow Flag, and I told Charley about my plans for a mile-long flag. He repeated everything Alice had said about the cops and Giuliani and a lawyer, adding a warning about the power of John Cardinal O'Connor and the Roman Catholic Archdiocese of New York. He cautioned that they might not allow the flag to go past St. Patrick's.

I repeated my concern that if I started bringing in lawyers to fight the city, the sponsors would freak and Cleve would walk.

"The sooner you make the flag," Charley said, "the better position you'll be in when all hell breaks loose." He offered to help me find a workshop, and he suggested I hire a helicopter to get an overhead photo of the completed flag. He could arrange that through his film connections. Charley gave me a hug and rolled out the door. Once he was back on the street, he yelled up to us, "Our flag in front of the cathedral—I love it!"

Alice and I went back to the fire escape. We were soaked through with perspiration. A big storm was building up in the sky. We looked at the montage of brown, orange, and rust colors washed across thousands of buildings. And black. Black everywhere. Shit and soot—those are the colors of New York. I loved it.

Before I left, Alice reminded me that I could crash at Number 9 when I returned. We could watch sports on TV, drink beers, and eat pizza. She gave me a peck on the cheek, sending me on my way. I grabbed a cab back to the hotel. Everyone in the lobby was wearing suits and dresses. I looked like a sweating pig. I held my room card in my hand so that security would know I belonged. Still, they watched me all the way to the elevator. Once in my room, I stripped and stood naked in front of the air conditioner. Then I slept.

———————

Late the next afternoon, I started pulling myself together to meet Franklin Fry. He was the head of Heritage of Pride, the official committee organizing logistics for the Stonewall 25 march. Cleve insisted that a letter of approval from Heritage of Pride to include the mile-long flag in the festivities was the key to getting Stadtlanders to finalize the project.

It was all up to me. Cleve wasn't coming; he would never put himself in a situation in which he might have to take no for an answer. Walking over to 666 Fifth Avenue in a suit to meet Franklin, I wondered if I was setting myself up.

"The Sixes" is a building so huge you can't see the top of it. It was a perfect place to meet Franklin Fry, who seemed more than seven feet tall. I picked him out in the crowded bar. We shook hands and he introduced Marion Belcher, a colleague from his day job. Franklin was only briefly disappointed that Cleve couldn't make it. We sat down and he reached out across the table, grabbing my fingers. "So, these are the hands that made the flag" he told Marion. "This is an honor."

Marion nodded but suddenly changed the subject. She hated that the bar was full of straight yuppies and suggested a change of scene. We left the Sixes and headed up Fifth Avenue to the Peninsula Hotel. Along the way, Franklin explained that the New York City Pride parade was the largest in the world. He was full of enthusiasm for the Rainbow Flag.

In the lobby of the Peninsula Hotel, there was a crystal chandelier as big as a house. The place had the feeling of old money. Richly paneled elevators took us to the top-floor bar and terrace. I ordered three drinks. The bill came to fifty dollars. We walked out to the rooftop garden and I looked over the bronze parapet. Fifth Avenue spread out twenty-three stories below.

I answered questions about Stadtlanders, responding to their immediate objections by stressing this was a pharmacy, not a pharmaceutical company. Still, Franklin saw them as a company making a profit on people dying. The message stung. Twirling the little umbrella that came with my margarita, I sipped the icy alcohol. On the cusp of twilight in a fiery glow, skyscrapers and spires cast sapphire shadows. The city lights turned on, glittering electric diamonds that outlined the vertical landscape. Enchanted metropolitan castles beckoned.

"You queens from California sure have a lot of nerve," Franklin joked. "So whaddya want from us?"

I explained the need for a letter of invitation. Franklin was willing to lobby his group to make it happen, but cautioned me, "When word gets out about this, you better be strong. There's some vicious queens in this town, and some of them would love to see you and Cleve fall flat on your face."

Franklin Fry is one of those people who has put his heart and soul into the gay movement. Even though this was business, it felt like I was making my first friend in New York City. We three toasted to success.

After drinks, Marion and Franklin walked with me toward Central Park, passing the windows at Harry Winston and Bergdorf Goodman. Franklin filled me in on the behind-the-scenes politics that made New York sound like a raging, chaotic mess. It wasn't going to be easy for an outsider. But it convinced me that once there was a real commitment from the sponsor, I was definitely moving to the city.

"Don't worry," Franklin said, giving me a big hug when we said our farewells, "this is going to happen."

Cleve arrived later that night and I told him the good news.

In the morning, we headed to Fire Island, a legendary playground for rich and beautiful gay men. We planned to meet the head of marketing for Stadtlanders, who was running a little store and information center in the Pines, the most upscale of all the communities strung along this thirty-two-mile-long sandbar. I would make a presentation and we would brainstorm on the project.

When the ferry arrived at the docks, Lisa Fischetti, Stadtlanders's vice president of marketing, greeted us and helped load our bags into little wagons. She was funny and bright, attractive, and the leader of the management team overseeing the flag production and promotion for Stonewall 25. We would answer to them, since they controlled the money. We pulled our wagons along the streets, which are really composed of boardwalks. There are no passenger cars on Fire Island. Deer roam wild. But everyone I passed along the way was gorgeous. I felt fat, forty, and invisible.

The place we would stay was a three-bedroom affair with two baths and a large living room that opened onto a deck with a swimming pool. The Great South Bay licked at the edge of a faded wood terrace that seemed to jut out over the water. I had heard rumors that Madonna used to stay here. But she never would have tolerated the tacky suburban interior, decorated in designer Kmart.

The three of us went to work after dinner. Lisa wanted to go over all the details. I was specific about my needs, including one assistant to help manage the seven thousand pounds of fabric. Lisa asked if I would be able to accomplish all that I had envisioned. Cleve assured her I could, adding, "She's the queen stitch bitch of all time."

Lisa laughed. She thumbed the glossy pages of my presentation, taking her time in looking over the aerial mock-ups of the proposed flag along Fifth Avenue. Cleve told her about my meeting with Franklin Fry and that his group would deliver the letter. All we needed was the pharmacy's commitment—and their agreed-upon grant of $250,000. Our plan was to leverage the symbol of our movement into something tangible we could use to fight AIDS. But we needed a name. After some brainstorming, we dubbed the project Raise the Rainbow.

Later that evening, Cleve and I went for a walk along the Atlantic Ocean to discuss the work ahead that would keep me in Manhattan for months. "I'm rid of you at last," he chuckled.

I flew back to San Francisco to prepare for the move. It was twenty degrees cooler than New York when I arrived. The porch of our group home was covered with plants and flowers. A thick blanket of fog wrapped around the hills as I fumbled with the front door. I turned on the shower to heat up the water and unpacked my bags. Dennis Peron, who ran the house, came down to my basement bedroom, wanting to hear all the news. "Did they give you the money?"

"Not yet, but they will," I insisted. I recounted the Fire Island negotiations with Stadtlanders. Dennis was amused that Pink Saturday and Pink Jesus hadn't been deal breakers. I told him I'd be moving to New York City in the early fall, probably staying at Number 9 while I searched for a workshop and apartment.

"You, princess—at Number 9?" Dennis laughed.

"It's not so bad," I lied. "Besides, it's not like I'm going to be there forever."

Upstairs, the French doors were open in the kitchen and friends crowded around the table. We went to say hi. Dennis told them that I hadn't received the money yet. I got skeptical looks.

"The Rainbow Flag is going to happen," I repeated.

"So how much are you going to get out of it?" one woman asked.

"Twenty-five thousand and housing."

"That's all?" she exploded. "What about Cleve?"

I explained that Cleve would get more as the consultant. But he also needed to sign up ten thousand volunteers. More skeptical looks.

"He's doing me a favor," I stammered. "Sure, there's strings attached, and maybe I'm just a marionette, Cleve's art slave. What can I say? I'm a whore."

In early September, I held a garage sale to bankroll my move. High heels were a dollar a pair. My dresses and costumes fetched five and ten dollars. Albums went for a quarter apiece. I took the earnings and bought several pairs of black jeans and black turtlenecks. They would become my regulation New York City uniform.

I cherished San Francisco, but now it bored me. The ballroom days were over. The Rainbow Flag was almost passé in this city, ubiquitous after fifteen years. I was broke. I needed money. And $25,000 seemed like a lot of money to me, especially for doing what I loved most. I also needed a new life. The move felt right.

I also believed Cleve's advice: to get anywhere in my career, I'd have to go to New York. Opportunity was knocking.

But for it to come to anything, the pharmacy had to be on board. Stadtlanders was flying in its top people to San Franscisco for meetings, the culmination of two months of planning. I focused on putting the finishing touches on our proposal.

As I finished packing for our flight to New York the next day, Cleve called. It was about an hour before we were supposed to be at a meeting with Stadtlanders for final approval on the project. He said he was sick and couldn't go with me. But he'd join the meeting by conference call.

Cleve was going to phone it in. The nerve. Was he getting cold feet? "So what's wrong with you anyway?" I said, trying to sound like I cared.

"I'm sick, sweating and throwing up."

What could I say? All this work together, and now Cleve's famous—and familiar—vanishing act. If this were anyone else and a quarter-million dollars were at stake, he'd drag himself off his deathbed. I wondered if I had embarrassed Cleve and he was cutting me loose.

But I gathered myself and dismissed all my doubts—and Cleve's—when I sat down with the Stadtlanders Stonewall 25 team. I quickly dazzled them. We got their commitment. I was officially hired to make the mile-long Rainbow Flag.

I left for New York the next day, assuring Stadtlanders, "No matter what happens with Cleve, I'll see this project through." I was determined that no problem was unsolvable. As I boarded the flight, I fingered a lucky thimble in my pocket.

17

Defending the Rainbow

It was late September 1993. I was standing in front of Number 9, holding two heavy suitcases and a shoulder bag, my arms and fingers slowly going numb. There was no doorbell, so entry was granted to those who screamed the loudest. I yelled my guts out to announce my arrival, rattling the top-floor windows of the building. Dana Beal finally opened the strange contraption of steel and wood that served as the door. I staggered inside the crumbling edifice, my burden tumbling from my exhausted hands.

"You're just in time," he said, bounding toward the stairs. "Johann is here. He's got some news about your press conference." He told me to head to the third floor, where Alice had coffee waiting. I looked around and suddenly recalled Dennis Peron's parting words: "Take a bottle of Kwell and watch out for the rats."

I splashed some cold water on my face, put on my tennis shoes, and headed upstairs.

Johann Moore, a veteran activist who always looked so skinny, waited at the top of the ancient stairway. He gave me a bony hug and handed me a joint. Alice gave me a mug of coffee. I gulped the warm caffeine. Then, Johann told me that tomorrow's Stonewall 25 press conference wasn't happening. I looked at him blankly.

"There isn't any money; the organization is broke," Johann said calmly. "People are pointing fingers at the event, saying it's a scam and doesn't stand for anything. A circus for corporate sponsors, only there aren't any sponsors."

"That can't be true," I stammered. I didn't tell him the pharmacy had cut a check for $10,000 to be listed as a major contributor.

"Oh, there's about $10,000 or $15,000 from a beer company," Johann said. "But all the money's gone. Office, salaries, travel expenses . . ." I wasn't surprised. Cleve and I had both gagged when organizers of Stonewall 25 announced a $4 million budget.

Johann told me activists were unhappy that Stonewall 25 lacked a political focus, despite the fact that the event was commemorating a riot by drag queens and street people. But organizers didn't want an ACT UP–type event. Alice had also learned that Stonewall 25 didn't even have a single city permit in hand yet.

Dana suggested that I go to the next ACT UP meeting to plead my case and garner their support, in case Stonewall 25' crumbled. He referred me to a woman named Ann Northrop, who often facilitated the meetings at the Lesbian and Gay Community Services Center on West Thirteenth Street.

"Her opinion matters," Johann said. "She's the conscience for a lot of the New York movement."

"Ah, she's a big pothead radical," Dana laughed. "Ann gets things done, that's all. She's trusted. You'll like her; she's our age."

Outside, I heard someone screaming up for entry. I opened the large broken window fixed with plastic and looked down. There was Vic Hernandez, the only other person I knew in New York. He shrieked, "Girl, I heard you were in town," parked his bike, and came up. He agreed that I should go to ACT UP. "I'll introduce you to all the girls. She is diva, and diva needs help." When Vic gave advice, he always referred to me in the third person, as if I were royalty.

Four of us, including Dana and Johann, crowded into a cab to the center. Vic dished on the ride over about fellow ACT UP members: who was a whore and who was an angel; who was dead and who was dying. I looked forward to the meeting.

ACT UP New York was the most famous source of radical queer activity in the world. Its outrageous antics were legendary. I had been in awe of the group since the December 1989 storming of St. Patrick's Cathedral. That's how activists protested the Archdiocese of New York's longtime meddling in city policy on AIDS education and condom access, as well as women's reproductive rights. Some chained themselves to pews while others shouted at the cardinal.

Its name an acronym for "AIDS Coalition To Unleash Power," ACT UP made an art of civil disobedience. It served as the playground of genius media manipulators, all thrusting AIDS into the public's face. A whole culture grew around the group, and Vic Hernandez was a big part of it. People regarded him as a shaman. When the epidemic worsened, Vic had decided to become a doctor and had left San Francisco to educate himself at Harvard.

The yellow cab wheeled up in front of the old brick building on West Thirteenth Street. A large crowd of people stood outside socializing and smoking cigarettes. Dana and Vic led the way through the throngs. People blew kisses toward Vic and glared at Dana, considered a troublemaker even by ACT UP standards. I stumbled, spastic-dancing, through the introductions and gossip. The main room was jammed with hundreds of queer folk. Just inside the front entrance, several long tables were pushed together and covered with literature—newsletters, pamphlets, flyers, all fresh from the photocopier. I placed glossy color flyers for Raise the Rainbow in a neat pile at the end of the pastel pulp buffet. They had already been inserted in a half-million gay publications, coming out the next day.

Dana came from behind, pushing me through to the front of the room until we stopped in front of a woman with silver hair, wearing soft blue jeans and a button-down Oxford shirt. "Ann Northrop, this is Gilbert Baker," Dana said, adding, "He's the one doing the mile-long Rainbow Flag."

Unsmiling, Ann looked directly into my eyes. "Oh yeah," she said with a flat voice. "So you're the one. I saw the ad in the *Village Voice*." I could tell she didn't like it. Dana began to recite my artistic accomplishments, but Ann stopped him. "I don't care about flags. It's a personal thing. Visceral. I never liked the Rainbow Flag, it's so . . ." Ann paused and then chose the next word carefully: ". . . icky."

She asked about Stadtlanders and told me she felt their underwriting was "sleazy." But Ann wrote my name down on a list of people who would make announcements at the beginning of the meeting. I would be given a chance to make my case. That was it. My project was unimportant. Serious issues demanded her attention. Ann finally smiled, and wished me good luck.

There was a racket as people sat down in metal chairs. The meeting was coming to order. From across the room, Vic waved at me, pinkie girlfriend style.

After several announcements, it was my turn to speak. Youthful men in worn black leather and antiquated Doc Martens looked up as I cleared my throat and made my pitch. I explained my vision. What it meant. Who was funding it. What it cost. I defended the fact that underwriting came from a pharmacy—stressing, as I had with Franklin Fry, the difference between Stadtlanders and a pharmaceutical company. When I finished, I scanned the room. The faces seemed unmoved.

There was a clear consensus: Rainbow Flag? Hate it.

During a break in the meeting, Ann Northrop waved me over. She was still smiling. "You're working with Stonewall 25? Well, maybe you could help us with some ACT UP banners for the march?"

"I don't think the Rainbow Flag will upstage ACT UP," I found myself saying.

Ann Northrop was tough but compassionate. I liked her. I left my first meeting of ACT UP New York filled with determination and vigor. Despite the chilly reception, I would make it a point to go back most Monday nights. Respect, I knew, is always earned, never demanded. While making a flag would be easy, community support was going to be a problem.

The next day I decamped from Number 9 and moved to Vic's place on the Bowery in Chinatown, a few blocks away. I rang the bell, and garbled electric sound waves signaled the opening of the heavy metal door. I climbed up a dingy staircase to the top floor, not that different from Number 9. Vic's roommate Eric, a small, serious young man, was on the phone. He waved me into the loft. Vic, he said, was on the other end of the line. He'd be late that night but would bring dinner. Vic was never on time.

Vic lived in a fabulous space. He had turned a Chinatown loft into a Lake Tahoe cabin—weathered wooden walls and polished oak floors, punctuated with a profusion of built-in cabinets. There were mahogany panels salvaged from a fancy library and a staircase, Addams Family style, where fine dust glimmered in mysterious shafts of light. Dominating the vast rustic salon were two giant naked marble gods. They had previously reposed in turn-of-the-century splendor on top of the abandoned bank across the street. The neoclassic figures were positioned at eye level so you could see them from every part of the room—even while doing dishes at the kitchen sink.

I settled in at Vic's place and continued planning the mile-long flag project, all the while preparing myself for the challenges I knew still lay ahead.

18

Russians, Bobbins, Flashbulbs, and Tears

A new press conference was scheduled for one autumn afternoon to officially kick off Stonewall 25 and the start of the international LGBT Olympics known as the Gay Games, both hosted by New York City. The event would also announce the mile-long flag. It began at 5:00 PM, across the street from the United Nations. Only a few cameras and reporters showed up. I stood with a representative from the pharmacy. Cleve, true to form, wasn't there. I was miffed.

The Stonewall 25 committee officials read a list of demands and announced the march routes and the lavish concert planned for afterward in Central Park. I was not asked to speak. I was embarrassed for Stadtlanders; the event was so rinky-dink.

The reception afterward at a nearby Hyatt hotel wasn't any better; tasteless food decorated a single tray on a large beige table in a hideous conference room with a bad view. People showed up, and I thought how lucky they were to have missed the collective fart the committee had blown for the media outside the UN.

At the reception, Franklin Fry asked me to say something about the Rainbow Flag. He led me over to the podium, where someone from the Gay Games had just finished remarks. I was brief and on message.

The pharmacy could count on me, despite this clown car that was Stonewall 25.

After I spoke, Franklin pulled me over to a pleasant-looking man in a tank top and blue jeans. He smiled at me. "Gilbert," Franklin said, "this is Richard Ferrara." The man looked flushed, out of place in a room full of suits, but his large brown eyes were very bright. I noticed they were the same shade as mine. Franklin explained that Richard made all the banners and flags for Heritage of Pride.

"I like the Rainbow Flag," Richard said. "It's an honor to meet you."

Our hands gripped firmly. I felt a spark.

"If you need any help," Richard said, "please call me. I know how to sew." He gave me his number, bowed, and walked away. There was something about him, such humbleness, and such massive grace.

"Thanks—that meant a lot to him," Franklin whispered. "You know, if you need an assistant, he'd be perfect."

I changed the subject quickly to permits, not admitting that I'd heard there had been zero progress. Franklin was unruffled, responding, "Oh, that stuff all happens later." I pushed further, asking whether the city officials knew anything about my proposed mile-long flag.

"There's the election, and everything is changing at city hall," he said. "We do things different in New York. Just wait."

The party was breaking up. I went into the hall and called home to San Francisco from a pay phone. I told Dennis there was a change of plans. I would be extending this trip. There were problems to work out.

Now that I had additional time in New York, I focused on looking for a workshop. I also scouted out local suppliers for flag materials. I took part in conference calls with Stadtlanders every few days. Cleve was patched in from California. I let him do most of the talking. But I made sure to take my own notes.

Progress was underwhelming. The ad campaign had not recruited the ten thousand volunteers we needed. Ten people had signed up to carry the flag thus far—and I knew all of them. We all rationalized that it was still so early, that the event was months away. So the pharmacy decided to order up another media blitz to spread the word. They also cut a check for $30,000 for the fabric. I was relieved. Even if they pulled the plug, I'd get the fabric delivery in a few weeks. Once I had that and a sewing machine, I could make the mile-long Rainbow Flag.

A realtor showed me a basement space in a high-rise in Chelsea, off Eighth Avenue, where I could set up the flag workshop. There was only a single window, but it was the best location at a price within the budget. And the landlord promised some improvements. The pharmacy lawyers would cover the lease. With those matters settled, I flew back to California to say good-bye and ship my life east.

Back in San Francisco, Tom Taylor had a surprise: he had tickets to the famed Bobbin Show in Atlanta. The annual event for hardcore seamstresses like me showcased the latest sewing machines by the top manufacturers. "Get real, queen," Tom told me. "You need special equipment. You're not sewing that mile-long thing on that piece of crap Singer 107."

In a heartbeat, the two of us were in Atlanta, joining thousands of people at the convention center, walking through huge exhibition halls. Acres of displays beckoned, offering every new sewing machine model available. We spent the entire day checking them out. Tom pointed out a high-tech contraption that fused together fabric with sound waves. It looked more like a big microscope than a sewing machine. There weren't any control knobs on the sleek, stainless-steel device. It had a sort of space-age, *The Day the Earth Stood Still* quality about it.

"Think of it," Tom said. "No thread to mess with, and so fast. You just guide the nylon and the machine does it all." He inspected the roller units that would hold the fabric and the guide wheels that automatically kept everything in place. This machine would allow me to sew at a far faster pace than I was used to.

The hyper sales rep showed us a piece of fabric sewn together by sound waves.

"How much is it?"

"This model is $12,000," he said, pausing, then adding, "without the computer."

Tom took a test-drive, wearing protective glasses and feeding short pieces of nylon under the nozzle where the sound waves came out and chemically melted the fabric together. He finished the small seam and tugged at the corners to show me its strength. Now I was intrigued. I put on goggles and took my place at the machine. I made a longer test piece and then handed one side to Tom and stepped back several feet with the other. At my signal, we both pulled. The fabric instantly came apart.

"Sound waves? I don't think so."

"Go ahead, live in the past," Tom said. "You're trapped in a horse-and-buggy technology."

While Tom did have a point, I stuck with tradition. I decided on a Union Special free-arm sewing machine that offered three continuous seams of real thread. The salesman put me in touch with the company's New York distributors.

Tom and I then went out for dinner. Over peach pie and coffee, I confessed my concerns about Stonewall 25 and the problems already evident. Things were less than luminous.

"Girlfriend," he said, soothingly, "you've got everything to make the big flag now. Let those other queens figure out how to fix the PR and volunteer recruitment. That's not your job. The pharmacy is loaded—and this whole project will cost less for them than one national television commercial. OK?"

Reading my mind, Tom asked what I thought about Cleve's inability to sign up volunteers.

"We'll figure something out," I said. "I have faith that if I build it, they will come," paraphrasing *Field of Dreams*.

Back in New York, Stadtlanders had finished negotiating a lease for the basement space in the Chelsea high-rise. It didn't have electricity, or a bathroom. One bare lightbulb connected to a long extension cord disappeared in a labyrinth of exposed pipes and steel reinforcement rods. A group of Russians was sent over to construct the workshop according to my specifications. The only one who spoke English was the leader, a burly man who called himself Jeff. I wasn't really certain if they were legitimate contractors, but they had tools.

Jeff went over the list of improvements: electrical outlets, bathroom, a paint job, some fluorescent lighting. He stopped dead at my request for a white linoleum floor. "You're crazy," he grunted in a Russian accent. "I'll get you some nice gray."

"I want white," I said, looking him squarely in the eyes. "Your work here was supposed to be finished yesterday and you haven't done anything." I handed him the yellow pages, repeating, "Find white."

Jeff thumbed the index and hunkered down on the dusty concrete with the phone, the only thing that worked in the space. After each call that led nowhere, he'd shrug. "See, what I tell you is true. Nobody has white. Everybody's got gray."

"It's in the lease, the floor is to be white," I pushed back. I showed him where the agreement read "white floor and staircase." Charley Beal had warned me about New York contractors.

"We're going to make a big flag, so huge it will fill up this whole room." My wrists flailed toward the far corners of the dank pit. "Just like a swimming pool, the fabric will touch everything, all the way up to here." I held my hand across my chest. "While I sew it, I have to look down the whole time. White will reflect more light."

Jeff argued that a white floor would show every speck of dirt, and would have to be cleaned every day. I told him I was prepared to do that. "Every day, polished to a gloss that I can see my face in clearly," I shot back. "So only white will do. Besides, my wardrobe is black." I was clearly scaring him now.

I pointed out where the staircase should be installed, to more easily move the finished flag out of the space. It would need a steel door thirty-six inches wide. When Jeff balked, I dug in; I insisted that the fire inspector would be here to make sure everything was up to code. I was lying, but his face filled with alarm.

"Impossible, but we'll see what we can do," Jeff said, giving in. "You and me work together, OK?" He snapped his fingers and the workmen shuffled around him.

The logistics of the project obsessed me. I spent my nights adding it all up. How much fabric could be sewn together at what rate, multiplied by ten thousand. How many days, how many hours, how many minutes. Then there was the weight factor, the massive volume, the number of folds needed to transport it. With one assistant, I would move more than seven thousand pounds, one handful at a time. The numbers were endless, like counting sheep. I'd wake up in the middle of the night worrying. I'd have another smoke, then begin adding up the numbers again.

Jim Ferrigan, the Paramount Flag expert in San Francisco, arranged to ship the fabric by Guaranteed Overnight Delivery. The company's trucks were decorated with their initials: GOD. He kidded me on the phone when I pressed him for a definite delivery date. "I talked to GOD this morning. Everything is under control."

The truck arrived on the appointed day. Refrigerator-sized crates were wheeled into the small elevator. One at a time, we moved eighteen of them down to the cellar and onto wood pallets. Each one weighed four hundred pounds. Working alone, I arranged the cartons color by color, and then inspected a sample box of each. The selvage edge had been milled to my specification—perfect in every detail. I pulled with all my strength and a few yards loosened from the heavy cylinders. Like that young boy dancing back in his childhood bedroom in Kansas, I wrapped some fabric around my body like a taffeta gown. It felt fabulous.

Mick Hicks and his lover Pete came down from Boston in a Jeep Wagoneer full of cameras and lights to take promotional photos for Stadtlanders. The Russians had done little work beyond putting up a wall of unfinished sheetrock and installing the steel door. Everything else was exactly the same as when I walked into the empty space three months earlier, including the lack of electricity. So we improvised, using lengthy cables to hook up everything to the power system on the first floor.

"We saw the advertising in Boston," Pete enthused. Mick's boyfriend was hot, intensely handsome with a dark mustache. "Everybody loves it. Very slick." But volunteer levels were still behind. They'd signed up only two people from Boston.

Mick opened up suitcases full of Nikons and lens attachments and set them up. I wanted him to record me starting the project. Pete helped set up light stands and arranged power boxes. Mick decided on colored gels for the shoot and Pete selected a sheet of indigo cellophane.

"Don't worry," Mick teased, "we'll do soft pink to make your skin tones richer. You're looking a bit gray, doll."

I excused myself to get dressed. We were still waiting for Cleve.

Cleve entered with a flourish, wearing a new backpack and parka. This was his first look at the workshop. He liked it. He asked if the pharmacy rep was still coming, adding, "I need a joint—I'm sick from the flight." Honestly, he looked terrible. Cleve always had a pallor to him, but he usually exuded such strength and vitality that one thought him generally healthy.

Cleve got cranky when he hadn't eaten, so I ordered delivery of chicken soup and a cream cheese bagel. "Throw in four double espressos and a piece of chocolate cake," I told the deli man.

Blood sugar levels sufficiently revived and a trail of pot smoke wafting around us, we caught up, gossiping about our friends and discussing politics. Cleve eventually relaxed. Mick and Pete busied themselves with the elaborate lighting.

"So the project's a mess," Cleve said with signature frankness. "Do they hate it here in New York?"

"Love and hate," I said. Ann Northrop's skeptical face flashed through my mind.

Cleve reported that San Francisco had a better reaction. "We've done it this time, girlfriend. People are blown away, green with envy."

I recounted the dismal Stonewall 25 press conference and the low volunteer levels.

"Maybe they'll just wait to the last minute like queens always do," Cleve said. "Fuck everyone else—they're all jealous because it's so fabulous.

"Whatever happens now, the pharmacy can't pull the plug," he added. "Once you make the flag, that's it. We both know our brothers and sisters in the struggle for liberation will carry it. Remember always that we're doing this for our people, not Stadtlanders."

Cleve lit a cigarette and took a drag. Then he confided, "There's trouble: the big kahunas on the company board of directors are freaked by all this money going to gay rights."

I pointed out that all the materials stressed support for AIDS charities.

"They're worried about a boycott from the Christian Coalition."

"We told them it would be controversial. I thought the pharmacy expected it."

"No shit, Sherlock. It's controversial even inside their own board-room now. I got them to give domestic partnership benefits to their employees and to institute a nondiscrimination policy." Cleve was amazing me yet again. "It's costing them millions," he grinned.

"Jesus, they must be expecting a lot from this."

"They expect a lot from you, so you'd better work, bitch."

A loud bang of the steel door announced the arrival of the pharmacy rep. She was young and pretty, with red hair. When she saw the yards and yards of fabric, her eyes twinkled. "Wow, this place is huge."

"Gilbert is going to turn it into a ballroom," Mick joked.

"He's not going to have time to dance," Cleve added.

"It's in my contract," I insisted. "Ten minutes of dancing every hour and loud music all the time. The Rolling Stones." Cleve hated them. "We're going to start at least a month late. I'm so restless, I have to dance." My feet made a pirouette.

"You guys are so outrageous," the rep laughed.

Mick began the photo shoot, arranging Cleve and me in front of a wall of boxes. We were dressed all in black. The six colors of the Rainbow Flag spilled out around us. Pete arranged them like a set director. Columns of fabric. Old Glory red, orange, Spanish yellow, emerald green, royal blue, and pansy purple.

"A little more red and blue in the background, Pete," Mick directed. "Perfect." He pushed a button at the end of a long cord he held in one hand. We were blinded in a flash of light.

Mick even coaxed Cleve into some extreme close-ups, with a weird reflector under his face. We were all so vain and joked about Vaseline and gauze, the tricks of movie stars. The session lasted nine hours. Mick would finish up a roll of film every few minutes and dispatch it for processing. The workshop was near the center of New York's photo district, so we got back the images quickly. The workshop floor was soon littered with Polaroids. I felt a wave of energy flow through my eyes.

"You're really in the moment, aren't you?" the rep asked me. "Cleve said you were like a movie star."

"Diva, not movie star," Cleve corrected her. "Gilbert is a legend in his own mind," he said, repeating his favorite dig. But Cleve had also given me the opportunity and tools to make the world's most beautiful flag. I thought back to how Cleve was there all those years ago when James, Faerie, and I put the first flags together. He was young then, a film student. I looked at him now, every crease in his face and every gray hair illuminated in Mick's lights.

Cleve *was* sick. In spite of the relentless Camille act, I could see it was serious. Somehow, since Cleve seemed so charmed and vibrant, I always thought he'd be the one to beat the odds. But behind the smile, he was fighting for his life. Cleve once told me he wanted to die in front of the White House. He gave strict instructions about how we should fly him to Washington, DC, and throw his body over the fence.

Cleve hated New York; it was cold and miserable. He tired so easily. But after dinner, he got a second wind and we hung out together, passing a joint and discussing scenarios for Stonewall 25. Things were in a good place. Mostly. The pharmacy rep was full of confidence about the project. Mick had dazzled everyone with his photos. But everything was weeks behind schedule. The workshop was still an empty room, an embryo dream. Cleve would still have to take care of his end of the deal: ten thousand volunteers. The next morning, I waved him off. Cleve hailed a cab in the snow on Eighth Avenue. He gave me a parting kiss—and a bitchy endearment: "Just remember, it was all my idea."

I was now alone, waiting for the Russian electricians. Christmas was only weeks away. There was the world's longest flag to sew—and only one Betsy Ross.

Dennis Peron came in from San Francisco for the holidays. We went up to Rockefeller Center to check out the Christmas tree and cruise the tourists.

"Gee, I never noticed how gay all this artwork is," Dennis said as he walked under a fresco of a man standing with his legs apart. "Such huge balls! I wonder if these shopping fanatics have any clue this whole place is one big boner."

Nestled in an underground café decorated in blond wood, out of the cold, we watched the skaters. "Did you hear about Cleve?" Dennis confided. "His eyes are giving him big problems."

"Well, is he seeing a doctor? You know how he is." I tried to dismiss it, but then I remembered how bad he'd looked.

"I think this is different," Dennis insisted. He loved Cleve dearly. He said Cleve worried that he might have CMV retinitis, which blinds people with HIV.

I assured Dennis that no one cared more about Cleve's health than I did. But now I was hearing that he might not be well enough to continue working, especially when the project was just underway. If Cleve didn't recover, I would be abandoned on this massive project, left solo, fighting with Stadtlanders. So I pushed back. "He hasn't done a goddamn thing for this project since he went home to California."

"Girl, you are so mean." Dennis glared. "Don't be a bitch! Can't you imagine how he feels, working on something he might never see? Show some compassion."

"We're all gonna die, Dennis," I sighed. I asked whether this wasn't another of Cleve's excuses to shirk responsibility. I brought up the failure of Pink Saturday. I talked about how Cleve typically enjoyed the acclaim but would back off from the hard work.

"And I'm telling you that Cleve is in no shape for this," Dennis said. "We're all real worried. If I were you, I'd be thinking of plan B."

Dennis and I walked through the crowds over to St. Patrick's Cathedral. Snow soon covered his silver hair. I lit a candle for Cleve and prayed silently. The irony of doing this in homophobic St. Patrick's was not lost on me. Still, I prayed with a heavy heart.

Afterward, outside on Fifth Avenue, Dennis gave me a kiss and a hug, then huddled his arms around me to keep warm. We looked at the sculpture of Atlas across the street from the big gothic church. The bronze icon towered over us, holding the weight of the world on his shoulders.

"That's how I feel," I said.

"Gilbert, someday this will all be over. Forgotten. The only important thing then will be your love for each other. Don't spoil the relationship, being a diva."

Ashamed of my cruelty, I decided to call Cleve.

When he picked up the phone, Cleve was fighting back tears. The doctors had found big spots on his vision, so they were testing for CMV. He was out of breath, plagued by colds, worried about pneumonia. He was canceling speaking engagements. I knew this time something was wrong. I wondered if this was Cleve's plan all along, to send me to New York as part of his final exit. Cleve joked that the mile-long flag would end up being his shroud.

I cried when I hung up the phone.

19

The Winter of My Discontent

While waiting for the Russians to complete the improvements on the flag workshop, I spent my days looking for my own place to live. I found a listing in the Sunday edition of the *New York Times*: a fourth-floor walk-up studio apartment. When I got there, I found four walls and a slanted floor. A little piece of sunlight made its way through the small bathroom window into the kitchen area, exactly five feet by five feet. But the selling point was that it was located diagonally across the street from the workshop. With winter raging outside, the convenience would be a luxury. I didn't hesitate.

They gave me the keys on Christmas Eve. I bought a Mr. Coffee and some cups. Dennis and Dana were my first guests. We had a tea party on the floor. It was so badly angled, you couldn't fill the mugs all the way or they'd spill over. Still, it was bigger than a hotel room; three people could sit down. Afterward, I invited them to the new workshop.

Snow had been falling for weeks. The Hudson and East Rivers had frozen. Even though the workshop was a mere half block away, a brief winter stroll required preparation. First, I put on Jockey shorts and a white T-shirt. Next, long-sleeved and long-legged thermals. Then two pairs of heavy socks. Blue jeans and waterproof boots. A down parka, a scarf, a sporty hat usually worn by homeboys, and gloves. It took more time to get dressed than to walk across the street.

When we opened the cold metal door, we saw a perfectly white tile floor. The Russians had also hooked up big banks of fluorescent lights that ran the length of the room. Dana turned them on and blasted enough wattage to illuminate a skating rink. The room was sprayed the same icy shade of white as the floor. The Russians had painted everything, even the pipes. It looked like Superman's Fortress of Solitude.

"Girl, you need some earth tones in here," Dennis advised. "What are these pipes for?" He pointed to the copper and aluminum maze that was suspended from the ceiling. "It looks like a submarine."

"The whole building is hooked up through this space to the street," I explained. "That's why we got a deal on it."

"Well, what happens if they break?" Dennis asked.

"No problem; everything is up on pallets. Besides, this high-rise is state of the art. Everything is first class."

Boy, was I wrong. A few days later, the temperature hit fifteen below and a twenty-inch water main burst under Seventh Avenue a block away. A wall of water two feet high gushed down Sixteenth Street, flooding every building. At seven thirty in the morning, I walked in to discover a pond of disgusting brown liquid covering the new floor. Miraculously, it had topped off just below the surface of the racks holding the fabric for the Rainbow Flag. I bought a big mop and a rolling bucket with a wringer and spent a whole day cleaning up the mess.

For New Year's Eve, Vic Hernandez invited me over for a party. "All the girls are coming," he said. "They all want to check you out." Vic would screen the movie *All About Eve*—in my honor.

Alice called up to warn me that it was two degrees outside, with a wind chill of thirty-five below. She had been invited to Vic's but was staying home. Late in the afternoon, I bundled myself up for the walk downtown. Light snow fell as I trekked through the Village toward Chinatown.

On Elizabeth Street, the final leg of my Arctic power walk, I passed a strange garden. At first it appeared to be a graveyard, but I got closer and saw the yard was filled with statues. Stone figures stood nude in the bleak storm. Every chiseled feature and muscular curve was frosted with white powder. The sight was so beautiful I decided to save up for a camera.

Chinatown was a mob scene of manic shoppers holding bags stuffed with produce. They squeezed into every inch of space on the sidewalk. The ancient pavement was covered with ice an inch thick in places. All was in slippery motion, people and things moving in an ooze of excitement and party cheer.

When I got to Vic's place on the Bowery, my moustache had little icicles on it. Vic had a fire going in every room—even the bath. The loft was lit by the glow of a zillion votive candles—his trademark touch from his San Francisco days. When the fog finally cleared from my glasses, I saw a room full of handsome men and a table set for a feast.

Vic hugged me close. He dragged me over to his four-poster bed in the alcove, threw me down, and rubbed his cashmere-covered chest across my face. "Gonna warm you up, girlfriend," he laughed as the guests looked on. "Everyone, this is Gilbert," he announced. "She is diva, and diva is making the Rainbow Flag."

His introduction was embarrassing enough, but then Vic stage-whispered, "I think you ought to get laid. That's the New York thing to do on New Year's Eve." I cruised into the kitchen behind him and was introduced formally, meeting again many faces from ACT UP meetings. Soon, the interrogations began.

One guy said he had heard that the Stonewall 25 organization was kicking out drag queens. There was already a protest scheduled in response. Another claimed that Stonewall 25 had thrown out NAMBLA to appease the United Nations.

"Stonewall was a riot, not a fucking trademark," Vic said, and snapped his fingers.

Listening to the barrage of questions and accusations, I realized these people expected me to offer an insider's view of the situation. But I didn't have a clue about the political mess they described. As far as I could tell, New York was giving the event one big yawn. And these seasoned activists were giving up; exasperated and cynical, they were writing off the twenty-fifth anniversary of the Stonewall riots. To make matters worse, Rudy Giuliani was set to be inaugurated as mayor in two days.

One morning, an old bicycle clanged through the door of the workshop, carried by a darkly handsome man who looked familiar.

"Gilbert? Richard Ferrara." He was the one in the tank top at the Stonewall 25 press reception. "I ride by here all the time and saw you'd started to make the flag."

"Just beginning. Please come in." I introduced my two coworkers. Ed was Cleve's assistant, running the front office. James McNamara, who helped make the original Rainbow Flags in 1978, was back sixteen years later to help build this one.

Richard looked around. "Wow, this is amazing. I thought you were going to have the flag made somewhere else; I never realized you were doing it yourself."

"Oh yeah, we're sending it out to a sweatshop," James laughed.

I explained that James and I were the seam-masters. Richard wanted to know if we needed any help. He reminded me that he had been making banners and flags for New York City Pride every year. I told him that we definitely needed his help.

I demonstrated for him. Red nylon slithered across the white floor and into the Union Special sewing machine. My hands formed a hem about an inch and a half wide. It's all in the fingers, sewing. Posture is important: butt on a good office chair, feet resting on two huge pedals, arms cradling the free arm of the complex mechanism. I took a deep breath and pushed down for power.

Vrrroommmm. Electricity shot through its copper veins and steel gizmos turned so fast I had little control. Slowly, timidly even, I pumped out staccato bursts of stitching that somehow ended up in a reasonably straight line. "It's like riding a dragon," I said, and then noticed a mistake. "Basically, I sort of hold on and let the machine do it all." The instrument whirred again and another four inches of fabric passed through the needles.

"At this rate, Gilbert will have just enough time to finish for Stonewall 50," James joked.

"Go ahead then, Miss Thing," I dared him, "I want to see you do it." James took my seat. He was very good, but soon the machine revved out of control and thread dangled from its jaws in a twisted knot.

I tinkered and tweezed the thread back into place. James ripped out the horrendous seam he'd made. Take two. I asked Richard to get the feel of it next.

"Oh, I couldn't," he declined with genuine humility. "I mean, it's your flag." But he offered to fold the fabric, kicking off his shoes to wade in. To complete the sock hop, James turned on the soundtrack to *Edward Scissorhands*.

And so Richard became a member of the team.

I would get to the workshop at seven thirty each morning, drink coffee, and start sewing. James and Ed would roll in around ten. Richard dropped by most evenings. The four of us put in long hours, often staying late into the night. To offset the cold of the constant winter storms, the Russians installed an old heater that kept us warm.

Ed was young and energetic. Every day, he'd have a fresh idea about how to get more people involved. But on the big map of Fifth Avenue he'd created to keep track of the number of volunteers to carry the flag, it was mostly blank. Cleve would call him with instructions from the West Coast. Ed took his assignments seriously.

But one morning, Ed approached me with a sober look. "Cleve's not coming to New York, is he? He's too sick and it's too cold." I told him that I didn't know. Hopefully, he would show up once it was spring. But we had to move ahead, anyway—with or without him. "Cleve's health is his number-one job now," I said.

Cleve's condition had deteriorated. While he didn't have CMV, he had pneumonia, shingles, and only five T cells. We'd talk every few days. Cleve was very brave, but I knew he was depressed, having been so sick for such a long time now. His life and friends were in California. New York was no place for Cleve. In stark contrast, I was full of energy, losing my gut, and looking good. New York was the best thing that ever happened to me.

There was still no community support for the mile-long flag project. We'd overestimated the public reaction. Our reputations and previous activist work weren't enough. Cleve grew more irritable as the scale of the flop set in. Yet the flag construction moved ahead of schedule, thanks to James and Richard. The flag was growing longer and filling the room as we worked in perfect tandem. The folding that Richard so graciously offered to do was getting heavier and taking longer all the time. Every few days, we'd all take off our shoes and socks to scrub and wax the workshop's white floor.

Rainbow colors filled the white room, lighting it up like a stage. When we sewed, passersby would stop and make frosty kisses on the window. Some thought we were making a hot air balloon. Children loved it. But I felt like a performing monkey sometimes.

Richard would bring us his homemade apple brown Betty and we'd order in some Chinese food. Johann Moore and his friend Jude Graham came by to help a couple nights each week. Vic made it over and Charley Beal dropped by. We all celebrated the completion of the first section of the flag. Six colors of the rainbow, thirty feet wide and eighteen hundred feet long. We were one-third of the way through making the mile-long banner.

New York was at the mercy of one of the worst winters in history. Blizzards closed everything. James was often snowed in at his home in New Jersey. Ed got the flu and I sent him home. Mostly alone during the day, I continued sewing as fast as possible and shoving the mass of completed flag into every corner of the room for folding later.

Richard faithfully returned each night, and the two of us would gather the day's work precisely into an orderly mound on the second of our three big tables. Richard had charm and wit. He was down-to-earth and without pretense. What you saw was what you got: strength, commitment, and the savvy of a native New Yorker.

One Saturday afternoon in late February, Richard took me over to the West Village office of Heritage of Pride. After we cleaned their floors, Franklin Fry showed me banners that Richard had created in previous years for the parade. I was impressed. A few days later, I approached Richard about sewing on my machine again. This time, I wouldn't take no for an answer. I showed him how to do it. He was intimidated at first, slow to get the feel for such a complex operation.

"Well, it's not as good as you or James," Richard said as he inspected his seam. He toiled a few hours each day, and got better as he went along. But something wasn't right; he didn't have our ease and grace. I finally discovered the problem: Richard was left-handed, and the machine was configured for a right-handed operator. Its design imposed a technical dyslexia on him. After he shooed me away, Richard focused in silent perseverance. He was quite nimble and finally mastered the machine, perfecting his technique.

In only a few weeks, we completed more than half the flag. February became March, and the snow continued. James eventually returned to his other job. I asked Richard about assisting part time, but he told me he was happy to stay a volunteer.

Speaking of volunteers, recruitment had stalled at a few hundred, still far short of our ten-thousand-person goal. Since the volunteers were going to bring in income by paying for carrying the flag, I wondered whether Stadtlanders would have to make up for the shortfall. Richard and Ed started dragging people into the workshop to see the incredible Rainbow Flag. It was a valiant effort on their part to boost volunteer numbers. From the gyms and clubs, from gay church groups and one-night stands, they lured them in. New friends and laughter filled the nights. Gaiety ruled, damn the uncertainties. Ed soon was filling in the blanks on his big volunteer map, one name at a time.

A week later, we had just begun work on the final third of the flag when the pharmacy scheduled a summit meeting in Manhattan for late May. Cleve would attend, if his health allowed. In our workshop, we hustled up the pace of sewing. I wanted to be done with the whole thing by the time of the meeting.

Meanwhile, there was more bad news about the Stonewall 25 committee. While the flag was almost done, they had not scheduled a single meeting with the city to discuss it. It seemed to me they were playing games with the city—and, worse, with the gay community. Mayor Giuliani's office called Stadtlanders, wanting to know what in the hell was going on. The red-haired rep from the photo shoot was assigned to do damage control. She flew up to meet with a flack in the mayor's office. After the meeting, she came to the workshop, took off her high heels, and told us, "We've been screwed. The city is mad at Stonewall 25 for not being up front. They're saying it's not going to be in Central Park but at Battery Park. I'm not sure I trust that committee. We should do our own communicating with the city from now on."

The mayor's office was also threatening to impose budget cuts on health services citywide. In response, ACT UP announced plans for a big demonstration on March 22 in downtown Brooklyn. That afternoon, Ed and Richard closed up the workshop early, and together we made our way on the subway to the protest. There were thousands of people, a profusion of banners and placards, and of course the police. I wanted to see firsthand how Giuliani's troops handled our community events, as a warm-up to Stonewall 25.

Richard ran into some friends and we joined their contingent; they were part of the ACT UP march scheduled to trek over the Brooklyn Bridge to city hall on the other side of the East River. Several blocks of a wide street were full of protestors, a human gridlock in a breathy steam.

Marshals with pink armbands gave a signal, and the big crowd shuffled forward. Red and blue police lights flashed against the golden twilight. A great buzz from the crowd swarmed through my ears— snatches of conversation, whistles, chants, and the roar of motorcycles all melted into an audio soup.

Up ahead, people turned left toward the bridge. We followed along, herded together, but something wasn't right. As we approached the concrete ramp, it became clear that the entire assembly was being directed into a walled portion of the roadway, where a huge riot squad stood before a line of paddy wagons.

The police were not going to let the march proceed any farther. They were making mass arrests. I jumped up on a retaining wall, thinking it was an escape, only to discover hundreds more police and empty buses waiting to take us all away. We were in a trap. Panic swept through the assembly. A giant formation of blue goons marched straight at us.

On the walkway, marshals from ACT UP were trying to keep people from climbing the fence to escape. "You will be arrested if you climb over the fence," they shouted through bullhorns. But thousands of people ignored the orders and began scaling the stone freeway embankments. The cops descended.

When the paddy wagons and buses full of people headed to jail, the police were left behind. They filled the very roadway we were just standing in. A sickening amazement oozed over me. There had been five or six thousand people marching. But Giuliani's thugs far outnumbered us. And their colossal force squashed us like a bug.

ACT UP was being sent a message from Mayor Giuliani. His get-tough policy and bad comb-over were both extremely Caesarean. The liberal mayors before him had accommodated the protests of nonviolent social justice activists. The new guy in Gracie Mansion was different. News coverage that night emphasized how the cops had stopped the protest march cold. This firmly established a new era of law enforcement—one of total control.

The sky darkened into a deep, pink glow. We headed back to Manhattan. Over the shimmering water of the Hudson, I could see the flicker of a torch—a dot of fire on the horizon. The Statue of Liberty still stood, thrusting a flickering lamp against approaching darkness. Yes, ACT UP was brave, our message righteous. But today, it was all about the men in blue. The police had had their way with us. They had stolen the spotlight away from AIDS and refocused it squarely on their new, aggressive style.

I worried what this would mean for Stonewall 25.

20

Clash of the Divas

Back in the workshop, it was a race against the clock. I was putting in fifteen hours a day. Richard gave us every free evening. Ed attended as many community meetings and events as he could to sign up volunteers. But not even a thousand were committed. The plan to raise a half-million dollars from the community, one volunteer at a time, had fallen short. Ed became Cleve's personal whipping boy. Everything the guy did was wrong. Cleve's hostility toward the project grew. And his long-distance micromanagement only added to my growing contempt.

I had been thinking about a new approach to fundraising: enlisting community groups to sign up their own volunteers to carry the flag. These groups would collect money from their own volunteers, then pay us a lump-sum donation for the honor of being mentioned in our advertising. During a conference call, I suggested the new strategy. Stadtlanders was dazzled. But Cleve hated the idea and slammed down the phone.

I fired off a company memo, blasting Cleve for his unprofessional behavior. I demanded he apologize to me and the pharmacy. If his attitude did not change, he should stay home and not come to New York. Just hours after I faxed it, the pharmacy called. I was chastised for being so mean; after all, Cleve had AIDS. Cleve had responded to my protest by playing office politics, and now he had the pharmacy in his corner. They had already felt my flamboyant nature and political leanings were liabilities. The top brass were unnerved that I turned every interview about the Rainbow Flag into a broader discourse on gay history and the role of political symbols.

Tension pulled from every direction. I felt squeezed, like a thread trying to fit through the eye of a needle.

The Stadtlanders pharmacy reps arrived at the workshop for the summit meeting at the end of May. They were ecstatic to find the Rainbow Flag almost finished, weeks ahead of schedule. Two giant sections rested on groaning tables as massive as grand pianos. The third piece, not quite finished, was neatly folded. The floor shone with a fresh coat of wax. Ed and Richard brought flowers and fruit.

The first order of business was my new fundraising strategy. An executive with big blonde hair told me that Cleve didn't think it would work. With great tact, I responded, "It won't work unless we try."

She brought up my memo, claiming it hurt Cleve and scolding me for infighting.

"Hanging up the phone in a conference call and throwing a tantrum are not acceptable," I told her, and watched as the big-haired blonde forced a smile. "Particularly when he hasn't done anything."

"Well, you know his condition. He's been sick all winter."

"Perhaps that's affected his judgment," I responded coldly. "Cleve is a hypochondriac. He's playing some kind of power game. His stubborn attachment to ideas he thinks he owns is childish. We're trying to fix it."

"Yes, but he's the leader, right?" She was nervous and wanted reassurance.

"This isn't about who's the leader. A real leader has respect for the work. Cleve wants to paint me as a temperamental diva on a star trip, a megalomaniac out of control. Well, he's wrong. I've done my job. The question is: Will he do his? Personally, I don't think he wants to."

"Oh, no, Cleve is working all the time on this now."

"No, he isn't. He has gone on a few big PR junkets, but he won't go out and work this one-on-one. That's too small for him." I let that sink in, then added, "I'm not going away, either. Cleve's counting on me to quit, walk out, but all I'm trying to do is help him. I'm committed to the Rainbow Flag."

The blonde had a pained look. She asked what I needed to go forward.

"Cleve should get off his high horse and get his butt to New York. The job is here, not in his bedroom at the Russian River. He ought to embrace this idea of enlisting existing groups and soliciting their support. After all, he's the one who could walk into a board of directors meeting and get their commitment."

"You're saying Cleve would be in charge of this wholesale volunteer recruitment?"

"His job is getting the volunteers, and time's running out."

"Interesting," she said.

Cleve soon arrived, just off the plane. Everyone took a break for introductions and a chance to look at the flag. Cleve asked to go to the hotel and resume the meeting later. But the pharmacy reps were eager to begin and handed out a briefing packet. On the list of topics for discussion was my new volunteer strategy. Cleve glared directly at me.

"I hate this idea." He wasted no time. "Gilbert, it's not your job to tell me what to do."

"It's only a proposal."

"No, it isn't. I know your little game, missy. Just don't start with me." Cleve bared his fangs. An uncomfortable silence filled the room.

The intensity of Cleve's anger made me nervous and fidgety. The pharmacy rep broke the tension by asking me to explain my idea. I did so, slowly and purposefully, in great detail. I stopped for pertinent questions and let the free flow of information and brainstorming gradually wash over Cleve. When we wrapped up, the pharmacy woman was very impressed. Cleve finally gave in; he dictated a letter to go out to all AIDS service agencies.

We took a break. Never had I enjoyed a cigarette so much.

———————

It was Memorial Day weekend. Under a clear blue sky on Eighth Avenue, strong gusts of wind scattered paper and laid waste to carefully arranged hairstyles. The big Chelsea street festival was getting started. Stadtlanders had arranged a table full of materials explaining the mile-long Rainbow Flag and the need for volunteers.

Charley and his boyfriend David Sellers rollerbladed circles around me as I carried a weighty sack with a portion of the flag. I planted it in the middle of the street. Richard arrived with a friend from the gym. Ed handed out clipboards and name tags to volunteers. Within minutes, we unfurled an eighty-foot section of the mile-long Rainbow Flag. It soared wildly above our heads in the stiff breeze. While children ran under it, we played tug-of-war with the seams, testing them for strength.

As the Stadtlanders reps applauded, I took a bow.

I knew it would require vast numbers of humans to tame the real thing, which would eventually measure 150,000 square feet and weigh seven thousand pounds. While the wind was an unknown factor, my math equations indicated that a bare minimum of twenty-five hundred people were needed to carry the Rainbow Flag. Cleve was in a dour mood as we discussed the physics of the project, so he wandered off.

After a while, I found him in front of a deli, finishing a cup of coffee and a cigarette. "So what's the deal?" I poked. "This thing is in trouble. What are you going to do about it?"

"Don't fuck with me," Cleve snarled. "I've had enough of you and that memo. You're an asshole."

"Cleve, I said I was sorry. But come on, you haven't done anything. What are you going to do?"

"Fuck you and fuck this flag," Cleve spat. "I quit." He started walking away.

"Oh, you quit?" I stomped out my Camel Light and followed him around the corner. "Right. Don't be ridiculous."

"No, you're fired," he yelled, slamming open the door to the Rainbow Flag workshop. "You fucked with me, and you fucked this whole thing up." Cleve was red with rage, throwing paper and kicking over furniture.

"Stop it, goddammit! You're being a baby," I thundered from the top of the metal staircase. "Get over it and get with it. Start doing your goddamn job!" Cleve wasn't the only one who could yell and swear at the same time.

Cleve grabbed a pair of scissors and headed toward the flag. "Fuck you and this shit."

"Don't you dare!" I shouted. He kicked the fabric violently, his fingers still knotted around the shears.

"Get out of here! You're fired, fucker," Cleve shouted. He threw the scissors across the room and they broke in two.

"I'm fired? For what—doing my job? Insubordination? Fuck you, you're fired."

"No, you're fired—you work for me." Cleve stomped his feet for emphasis. "This is my project. Get out."

"I'm not your art slave."

"You're fired!" he screamed again, as loud as he could.

"No, you're fired!" I said, matching him decibel for decibel.

"You're fired!"

"You're fired!"

The door opened and the sweet redheaded pharmacy rep came running in.

"Oh my God," she said, almost in tears.

"Go away. This is personal," I told her.

"You guys work this out, OK?" she pleaded.

"He's fired," Cleve insisted. "Tell everyone he's fucking fired."

The rep gasped and disappeared.

"You're the one who's fired," I countered. "You insult the movement with these antics. Go home! I don't need you."

"Fuck you! I'll destroy you! You're fired!" Cleve was even more enraged now that the pharmacy rep had witnessed his tantrum.

"You're fired!" he thundered.

"*You're* fired!" I thundered back.

When the pharmacy rep returned, she looked at the workshop in shambles. "There's your flag," I told her. I walked out before she could say a word, shaking with fury, and headed to my apartment.

A cold shower brought me down a notch. I phoned the workshop and the pharmacy rep answered, speaking in hushed tones. I could hear Cleve in the background, still ranting. I headed back out, breathing deeply and walking fast, all the way through the Village toward Number 9. On Broadway, I bought a couple of beers. On the news racks by the checkout counter, a tabloid jumped out at me. GUINNESS BOOK OF WORLD RECORDS! 300 LB. BABY! It included a doctored photo of the fattest human being, crying in diapers. The Rainbow Flag was supposed to go into the *Guinness Book*, but given this kind of crap, suddenly I didn't care.

At Number 9, Alice opened the brews and I spilled out the whole story of our fight. I wondered if Stadtlanders would fire me.

She commiserated. But she also had news. "You'll probably die when I tell you this. There's a story in tomorrow morning's paper about the city and Stonewall 25. You're fucked."

"God, don't tell me."

"Oh yes, the whole thing is going down FDR Drive to the Battery. It's official—no Central Park and no flag on Fifth Avenue. The city is sending a million people to walk on a covered freeway."

"Shit. And the Stonewall 25 people?"

"Watch and see; the city can make them do anything now. Stonewall won't sue, so they won't win."

"Great," I huffed. "Not only am I fired, the flag doesn't happen."

"Fuck the city and this pathetic excuse for organizers," Alice fumed. "You know, just do it. What are they gonna do—stop hundreds of thousands of people from going up Fifth?" I tried to imagine that as Alice continued. "The whole point of the parade in New York is that it goes by the cathedral. The gay community fought for years to be there. But now here comes the new mayor and it's the first thing he takes away."

I called the offices of Stonewall 25. Franklin said they would fight the city on the new route but wouldn't go to court. Fools. He assured me that a deal was being worked out behind the scenes. A possible compromise was that the mayor's office might give us First Avenue, going past the United Nations to the Great Lawn in Central Park. But what about Fifth Avenue? I asked. Franklin said the city's offer meant that the flag would be unfurled around eight o'clock in the morning— when no one would be there.

As I hung up, a tingling vibration covered my skin and I felt my face sag.

Alice swigged the last of her beer. "It ain't over yet," she said. "Some people are talking about an alternative march."

On my way back home, I passed the workshop. The lights were on and I looked through the window. Cleve and the blonde pharmacy woman were cleaning up the mess. I noticed they were going through all the boxes and file cabinets, looking for something.

The next morning, I woke early and went to the workshop. When I checked the computer, I discovered that my memo about Cleve's tantrum had been deleted from the hard drive. The flag was a bit of a mess, but everything else was spotless and rearranged. The pharmacy rep arrived. The atmosphere was cold.

"Cleve left this morning," she said softly.

"Without even saying good-bye? That's outrageous."

"Let's go outside for a walk," she said, leading me up the metal staircase. My footsteps echoed off each steel step. I wondered if this would be my last time at the workshop. She bought us both coffee to go and we found a stoop in the sun.

She expressed her disappointment over our battle scene yesterday. I held firm, pointing out Cleve's behavior. I suggested that it was OK if Cleve left, since I was doing both his and my job. She was shocked at my stance. I told her to keep Cleve on as a consultant but just give him another job that didn't involve the Rainbow Flag, which he clearly didn't care about. She said she'd think about it.

But she had another issue to air. "Listen, about you wearing dresses in the workshop . . ." She wasn't missing a beat. This was stinger to stinger.

"So, what?" I tensed, waiting for her explanation.

"We don't think that's such a good idea. I mean, what if the media came in and saw you like that?"

"What exactly are you saying here?"

"It doesn't fit with our corporate image and it detracts from the AIDS issue. Don't do that in the workshop."

"You're out of line," I lashed back. "I always dress to look professional. If I decide to wear an evening gown when I'm sewing, big deal. I'm not sure you have a clue what Stonewall 25 is all about. Drag queens, that's what. It is not appropriate for you to ever tell me what to wear. What would the press have to say about that?"

I let the implied threat hang there.

"Thank you for sharing that with me," she said, swallowing hard.

"You're not the only one who's disappointed," I said, staring as hard as I possibly could into her eyeballs.

"Oh, guess it's time to go," she abruptly said, fumbling with her watch. Her colleague, the sweet red-haired one, arrived and brought their bags. I helped them into a taxi. With brave smiles plastered across the faces of their elaborately coiffed heads, they waved good-bye.

I wasn't fired. At least not yet. When I walked back to the workshop, Richard and Ed were waiting. Richard finally agreed to sign on as my assistant so we could finish the flag and get it on Fifth Avenue. I felt a ray of light shine on me. I decided not to tell them about the latest decision from city hall.

I plugged in the machine and hung new spindles of thread. Richard started folding up the scattered fabric. Ed worked on writing letters. Then I opened up a box under the sound system and pulled out a pair of silver high heels.

My clothes fell to the floor with record speed. I donned a black sequin chiffon evening gown that fell off one shoulder. My hands adjusted the silver Barbra Streisand wig. Suddenly, I was a new man. In my heels, I was six feet, five inches of pure glamour.

Resuming my place at the sewing machine, I fired away with a fresh intensity. We listened to the Stones' "Paint It, Black" at a loud volume. Richard and Ed smiled but didn't say anything, not wanting to cross a diva in high fury. My fingers worked in time to the dervish musical beat.

"Oh my God! She's been driven to drag!" Charley Beal declared as he appeared at the top of the staircase. "Alice told me everything. So are you fired?"

"Not yet. But they don't like my dress."

"If you're not fired now, they're not going to fire you."

"Maybe."

"They don't have any choice. After all, you made the flag and you're in New York. I think your position is very good, especially right now. Stonewall 25 is a disaster. The only interesting thing going on is the Rainbow Flag. You should fight for your vision and the freedom to express it."

"The pharmacy doesn't have the balls to go to court on their own," I said. "And now, with Cleve hating me, I don't see how that's going anywhere." I jumped onto a huge pile of cloth and looked up at the infinite ceiling.

"If I were you, I'd keep making waves," Charley advised. "Remember the ancient law of politics: the squeaky wheel gets the grease."

"Or," I shot back, "it gets replaced."

21

An Affair to Remember, a Night to Forget

I had made a date—but not a date, really—to meet Richard Ferrara on the observation deck of the Empire State Building. It was raining and my shoes made squishing sounds as I walked through the granite lobby. People stared, but I didn't care.

Admit One, said the yellow ticket stub with serial number 2113703. I stared at this crude piece of paper and wondered what I was doing. Maybe it was better to maintain a platonic friendship with Richard and focus on working together to create the flag. After all, Richard's joy toward the project gave me hope. I needed some of it at this time, as the challenges from the mayor's office increased.

The elevator ride to the top was bumpy, shuddering to a stop on the eightieth floor. When the doors opened, I was greeted by someone in a King Kong suit directing me to another set of elevators up to the eighty-sixth floor. I was right on time, exactly 10:00 PM. But Richard wasn't there yet. Torrential rains were still falling. After about fifteen minutes of waiting, I had to pee; all that coffee back at Number 9 had my kidneys working overtime. But I didn't want to miss Richard, so I lingered in the gift shop, thumbing through postcards and fingering tacky souvenir cups and building replicas, while keeping a nervous eye on the elevator doors.

At 11:00 PM, I figured something was really wrong. Richard was usually very punctual. I called his apartment but only got the machine. My bladder was burning. I asked a guard for the restroom. He said it was all the way down where I bought my ticket. I told him I wouldn't make the trip downstairs in time. He just stared at me blankly. Another guard nearby took notice. He checked out the Rainbow Flag on my jeans jacket and the gay pride button. He told me to follow him and walked me back into the gift shop area. We passed a postcard kiosk in the corner and he unlatched a small door that opened onto the north side of the observatory, currently being renovated. He smiled conspiratorially and walked away. I waited until no one was watching, then slipped through the doorway. I was backstage at the Empire State Building, alone on the eighty-sixth floor.

I looked for a bathroom, but there did not seem to be one. My feet kept stumbling down the corridor to an opening at the bottom of the terrace. All the glittering lights of Gotham spread out before my eyes as far as I could see. To the east, the lights were on at the United Nations Building. To the north, I saw Rockefeller Center lit up. Rain washed my squinting eyes as I tried to make out St. Patrick's Cathedral amid the low, dark clouds. My feet came closer to the edge until I was looking down.

"I'm a fool for you, New York," I said, laughing madly. Unable to handle the pressure any longer, I unzipped my pants and pulled out my dick. My bursting bladder shot piss out over Manhattan. Lit up by the glare of a million watts, a river poured out of me.

Raising my face up into the rain, I let out a long, deep breath. I was beaten. New York had won. Everything I had worked for was out of control. Community response was dismal. There wasn't anything I could do about the bureaucratic dickheads at city hall. The Stonewall 25 organizers were cowards. I could lose the mile-long flag project. On top of all that, I was in love with Richard.

I knew this was a pinnacle moment. My body relaxed and I got into the phallic cosmic-ness of it all, just holding my penis long enough to become slightly aroused. It felt good standing on top of the Empire State

Building, asserting my sexuality. Putting the mile-long Rainbow Flag up against St. Patrick's Cathedral was a big dick contest. Our symbol would be bigger than their symbol. I could barely make out the spires in the cloudburst. My penis, their phallic towers.

If Stonewall 25 failed, it would have ramifications that would shake our community beyond New York City. The mission of enormous gatherings like this was to empower us. The energy from these events was supposed to spread our message far and wide. I wasn't alone in thinking this latest mess could mark the end of our movement.

Standing at the edge in the rain with my pants unzipped and dazed with revelation, I imagined that I looked like the tarot card the Fool, about to fall off the building. As fresh water from the sky cleansed my hair, I thought of Richard. Explaining this latest twist of events from city hall would enrage him. Richard was surely an angel; he had deep principles and injustice was a personal thing with him.

Slippery fingers zipped up my soaked blue jeans and I treaded back through the construction debris. I waited at the doorway, peeking until all eyes were turned away, then popped back into the gift shop. Richard still wasn't there. A clock chimed 11:30. I had been waiting an hour and a half.

I suddenly remembered the movie *An Affair to Remember* with Cary Grant and Deborah Kerr and how they vow to meet at the top of the Empire State Building to seal their love. But an accident intervenes and she doesn't arrive. I began noticing other people hanging out, and wondered if they were all waiting for a lover or friend who never comes.

Gay liberation is a visibility thing. That is our whole struggle. Just to exist. It's about symbolism, like waiting on a friend at this icon of American culture. It's about wearing a Rainbow Flag and a gay pride button defiantly. We tell people we are everywhere, even here, at the top of the Empire State Building. It's the ultimate button we push every day in our lesbian and gay lives. Power is when we say, "I'm gay."

Minutes fell heavy and the rain ticked against the windows. New York City had me tangled up in blues. Richard wasn't coming. The guard that had been so kind announced that the building was closing.

Silently, I descended in the elevator, the last few floors swooshing by in numerical lights. The doors opened and my ears popped. The building lobby looked like a mausoleum, all cold and polished. I hailed a cab in the rain. The blur of lights and wet streets made every tear a diamond. I said a little prayer for Richard.

The next day, I learned that Richard had been there all along, trapped by crowd control on the eightieth floor. He waited an hour before finally leaving, mad that I had stood him up. Friends and lovers should never meet at the top of the Empire State Building. *An Affair to Remember* has ruined it for ordinary people with everyday passions.

22

Last Shift at the Sequin Mine

I was right about Richard; he was furious when he heard the Stonewall 25 people were going to cave in to the city. We were just the seamstresses, kept out of the loop of power that would decide the fate of our beautiful creation. I told him bluntly, "We've been sold out by everybody."

But Richard would not sour. He insisted that we get back to the task at hand. His optimism defied the situation. "You sew, I'll fold," Richard declared, snapping me out of the blues. After a few minutes, the sewing machine was running at the maximum speed, foot to the floor. Fabric peeled away from the wheel at the end of the presser foot. Stitches flew from my fingers like sparks. I always believed that sewing was butch, right up there with welding. The fabric piled up quickly. Once in a while, I would look up and see Richard dancing around the vast stack. He spun it this way and that, carefully straightening each fold into place. The two of us worked silently, letting our hands move the moments forward. When we tired, we changed places. He would sew, very well now, and I would fold. We got high on stamina. Concentrating on the task before us was the best thing. The politics would sort themselves out later.

As the last red stripe slithered off the machine and coiled into the Rainbow Flag, Richard and I marked the milestone by taking photos. We then wrestled the three-and-a-half-ton load into a precise mound of seams. We only needed to join the three giant sections together and it would be complete. We decided to save that task for the next morning. Richard grabbed his bike and we headed out the door. Another shift at the sequin mine was over.

I headed downtown to Number 9. Alice was waiting with another news clipping, which showed a map of the two proposed march routes. We read and reread the article explaining the city's concern for overcrowding in Central Park.

"They're out of their minds," Alice snapped. "How can the Battery be bigger than Central Park?"

"That's good," I said. "We'll probably get Central Park now, because the city looks stupid and mean. But this First Avenue thing is bothering me. I didn't design this flag to go on First. And there isn't enough room." I got a ruler off Alice's layout table and held it up to First Avenue on the map. "The march route isn't even a mile long."

"Amazing—your flag is too big for New York City," Alice laughed.

"Now, on the other hand, Fifth Avenue is almost twice as big," I said. We calculated the physical space taken up by a gathering of one million people. We even estimated how close they would be standing next to each other, given humid weather. Our math would prove that the mile-long Rainbow Flag did not belong on the Battery or First Avenue. A march on First Avenue could result in a crush of people, a possible stampede, and even fatalities.

Suddenly, we jumped up at the same time, lifted into a floating revelation. Our mouths screamed in unison, "It's not safe!" The city was liable for the public safety! Marching on First Avenue would risk casualties and hundreds of lawsuits.

We rechecked our math. The safety issues were proven over and over again. Alice put all the yellow legal pad pages in a manila folder. "Should I call the *New York Times* now?" she asked, twirling a Rolodex. "Here's Bill Kunstler's number and one for the NYCLU. For the press conference, let's have Charley arrange some ambulances as a backdrop."

"Not yet," I said. "We should wait. Mercury is still retrograde. And this is too good a salvo to waste." I deposited this powerful information into my memory banks for later withdrawal.

The flag workshop looked like a million bucks, thanks to Richard's resourcefulness and the generosity of another friend and frequent volunteer, Robbie Tucker. Between the two of them, a comfortable environment full of thrift-store furniture welcomed me each day. Richard had advised me, "If you want a lot of people involved, have a good clubhouse."

I also liked to be there alone late at night. With the music up and the lights on low, I'd labor over the Rainbow Flag, tweaking the seams and folds into perfection. Sometimes, I would fall asleep during an all-nighter, waking up on the mountain of cloth.

One such morning, after a workshop sleepover, I was jarred awake by the door buzzer. It wasn't even 7:00 AM. In my stupor, I fumbled for my clothes and the keys to the front door. The steel staircase was cold against my bare feet. It was the perky Stadtlanders rep with red hair. She held a large suitcase. "I couldn't get my key to work," she apologized. "What are you doing here so early?"

"I worked till around three and I guess I fell asleep. Sorry I look so awful." My hair was messy and I had morning breath.

"Stadtlanders sent me up to work with you guys," she said with a sincere smile. "I'm here for the duration."

I had suddenly been assigned a full-time supervisor? I couldn't absorb the news right away. I begged off for an hour to go home to shower and change. When I returned to the workshop, newspaper and coffee cup in hand, I was wearing a nice polo shirt and creased jeans. I took my turquoise swivel power chair and tried to look casual, opening my interrogation with an offhand "So what's up?"

"We're freaked out about the project."

"You're here to fix it? What about Cleve?"

"He's not coming. He's too ill to travel."

"So is he out, or what?"

"We've decided to manage everything from company headquarters. It would be a disaster if any of this got out to the press. We have to protect Cleve; he's too important to the movement. We're counting on you to be the consummate professional you've always been." She was soliciting my support for a preposterous cover-up.

"So who's in charge?"

"We're collaborating, right? You're the artist. You've done brilliantly, beyond all expectation." She paused. "But Cleve is the one who brought this to us. We'll all pitch in to make sure the job gets done, since he's not here."

I offered her a cigarette and we adjourned to the sidewalk. "Is it going to work?" she asked point-blank. I sensed this was the real reason for her visit.

"Yes, if it's done right." I exhaled blue-gray smoke.

"We're going to do everything to make that happen," she said. "Stadtlanders has a lot riding on this. We want you to know that we're putting our faith in you."

"But not the reins?" Another plume of exhaust trailed from my lips. "So what do I do now? The flag is done." Our gaze followed the one shaft of morning sun through the window to the Rainbow Flag in golden slumber.

"This has to work," the rep said with the voice of someone whose job was on the line. "Help us. Please."

Realizing my advantageous position, I seized the moment and demanded full control of the mile-long Rainbow Flag on Pride Day. I needed to supervise the task of positioning and unfurling it. The red-haired woman agreed.

But I needed to explain something else to her. "Sooner than later, something like this goes out of control," I said. "Everybody lets go—even me—and it takes on a life of its own. That's the transcendent power of the moment. But I'm not letting go of the flag until I'm sure she's flying. This is Kitty Hawk. Count on me to do all humanly possible to achieve my vision." My hand grasped hers in friendship.

I then told her everything I knew about the situation with the city and the Stonewall 25 organizers. She was flabbergasted. She pulled out a legal pad and started taking notes in pencil, then asked whether we should go to the press with this bombshell.

"Maybe," I said. "Think of the headlines: City Tramples on Rainbow Flag AIDS Drive. You'd be heroes if you stood up to them. Why be the victim of government and corruption, when you can be the agent of change?"

The woman suddenly lost color in her face, explaining that Stadtlanders didn't want to be placed in a political position. They would prefer to negotiate with the mayor's office.

I lectured her on the integrity of fighting rather than caving in. I suggested that agreeing to First Avenue amounted to a desecration of the Rainbow Flag. "Ideologically, this is a fight-or-die situation," I railed on, my voice growing in fury. "The stakes are higher than the fate of this one flag. This isn't about where the Rainbow Flag goes, but how the gay and lesbian community fits into society—and under whose terms."

The rep offered a frozen smile in response to my screed.

I suggested the flag join the illegal activist march being planned for Fifth Avenue. I showed her the map I made with Alice and explained that Fifth was a better fit for marchers than First. I realized I needed to prove my point more concretely.

"Let's cruise," I said, rolling up my charts. Grabbing a tape measure and a raincoat, I led the rep outside. We were going on an adventure. A cab took us to the United Nations. On the way, I watched as the rain washed over the streets like liquid glass. Red lights from the tails of automobiles reflected crimson, luscious and wet, that seemed the ultimate lipstick color.

When we jumped out of the cab, I led her to the pedestrian bridge. "People could fall off of this," I pointed out. "Look how the roadway narrows." Indeed, First Avenue was a jungle of exit and entrance ramps. The area in front of the United Nations Building was a hodgepodge of bad '60s landscaping. At the bottom of the long traffic ramp, I pulled the tape measure from my raincoat and gave her one end. When the traffic light changed, I ran across to the other side of the street with the metal strip. I hollered back, "How long is it?"

"Twenty-nine feet, six inches," she yelled back. The Rainbow Flag measured thirty feet across. I crossed the street and rejoined her. She frowned. "So," she asked with uncertainty, "we could squeeze?"

"The flag is flexible," I said. "That's not the problem; it's the crush of bodies I'm worried about."

"Crush of bodies? Like at a Who concert? That would be terrible."

I pulled the morning paper from my back pocket; there was a horrific article about hundreds of Muslims stampeded to death at a religious festival. "It happened today and could happen tomorrow. We've got a problem here."

As we stood in the downpour, I suddenly flashed back on the 1991 Christo installation in California where a woman was killed by a giant umbrella. She died for art. "I may be indulgent, even derivative," I told her, "but I won't be negligent. As your creative consultant, I advise you that First Avenue is unacceptable because there are too many safety hazards for public assembly on the scale everyone expects."

"We're stuck," she responded. "We'll have to do what the city tells us."

"No you don't."

"But sometimes you have to go along to get along," she said, lighting a cigarette and exhaling smoke and bewilderment.

"We're marching to different drummers," I said flatly. "I'm going to do what's right for me."

"And that is?"

"I don't know. Yet."

23

A Bump in the Road

A few days later, Johann Moore and Jude Graham came to the workshop to help me cut string into small lengths. These ties would secure the huge flag when it was rolled up, thus making it more easily transportable to the parade. The plan was to feed it, foot by foot, out of the back of a truck to the volunteer flag carriers. Strategizing over this engineering challenge had cost me a great deal of sleep before I found a solution.

Over a period of hours, mounds of white cotton cords piled at our feet like hair around a barber's chair. "How many more do we have to make?" Johann complained. "My hands are getting blisters."

"Uh, three thousand," I mumbled.

The tedious process of bundling the Rainbow Flag was underway. I had estimated the entire process would take eighteen days. "When we're finished," I told them, "we have to stack the coil back onto the huge table—with no twists. The margin of error on this is zero."

Richard arranged the tables at the far end of the room for the procedure.

I instructed my team on how to fold the flag. My arms reached wide, reducing the cloth into a smaller and smaller width. I showed how, when rolling it, to make sure the two outside seams are always visible. That would fix any possible twists in the fabric. I held a firmly packed cylinder of fabric in my hand, about the diameter of a big fire hose. "The strings all get tied into perfect bows that instantly untie, to unfurl the flag."

Jude put her finger where the string crossed itself and I made a bow. "It's magic," she said as she pulled a string on one of the bows. The cord slipped away faster than a rodeo rope trick.

"And only ninety-nine thousand more to do," she laughed. "Eighteen days? You mean eighteen years!"

We were all elves in the fairy-tale factory, debating how to screw in a lightbulb. Johann put on some Boy George music. After some experimentation, we improvised a synchronized hand-and-wrist ballet. Within a few hours, the monotonous repetition had our upper extremities aching. We felt more like meat packers stuffing the world's biggest sausage, the flag being tied into a long chain of colored bologna.

On the second day of bundling, Richard and I decided to take a lunch break and get some sun on the Christopher Street Pier. The rotting wooden pilings of the pier swayed in the river current. We felt the subtle movement under our deli sandwich picnic, like a lazy hammock, swinging back and forth. The lull of the afternoon settled into my bones. I had made a new friend in Richard. Yet I was losing an old friend: Cleve. The never-ending dualities of fate tore at my conscience.

Cleve was someone I cared about. Hurting him and humiliating him into leaving the project bothered me. Now, empty silence and a cold shoulder were all I ever got from California. Cleve spoke to us solely through Stadtlanders.

That night, the assembly room of the Lesbian and Gay Community Services Center filled with reporters. The Stonewall 25 committee arranged themselves behind folding tables to face the media. Elected officials and a who's who of New York City community leaders were also in attendance. I was given a seat on the far end. Richard and Jude hung a section of the Rainbow Flag from the exposed pipes overhead for a backdrop.

The press conference began and the announcement was made: the revised parade route would be along First Avenue. A chorus of boos and obscenities erupted from the audience. Reporters began shouting questions all at once. The Stonewall 25 committee put on a brave face.

Tom Duane, a gay city council member with HIV, offered a dissenting voice. "We're getting pushed around by the mayor's office, but I'm marching up Fifth Avenue." Reporters jumped at the news of an alternative march.

A man reporting for the *New York Times* pulled me aside, asking what would happen to the mile-long flag. I told him it would go on Fifth Avenue, one way or another, just as a Stadtlanders women tugged at my sleeve to stop the interview.

Eventually, I wandered out of the center into the cool night and considered my options. Everybody's ominous warnings of the difficult political climate in New York City had come true. Mayor Giuliani was not poised to negotiate with us. Rather, he would rule by decree. We were officially fucked.

The next morning, in a last-ditch effort to save the project, I composed a memo to the Stadtlanders CEO and the top brass. I declared that I would not be liable for any fallout should the flag be moved to First Avenue. In fact, I stated, there was such a massive risk to public safety that it would be better to not do it at all.

At a company meeting in the workshop later that day, I tried to state my case again, pulling out my maps and documents. The top pharmacy man listened, but I knew it was useless. For all their charitable intentions, Stadtlanders didn't have a clue about what the flag meant. Nor did they want to know anything about gay rights. This was a marketing gimmick, a way into the pockets of people with AIDS. Their only priority was to cover their ass and their investment.

The executives were planning next to head downtown for a rendezvous with the mayor's people, scheduled in half an hour. I gathered up my materials, intending to join them. But the big cheese from the pharmacy did not want me to attend. He said I was too political for this kind of business, that there would be no place for art and passion at the business table.

The next day, I was messengered a new Stadtlanders contract. I was ordered to sign it immediately. It contained clauses about not stirring up trouble, and petty points about media management and possible punitive actions if I disobeyed, including forcing me out of the workshop and my apartment. It enraged me. This was corporate censorship and intimidation.

Charley Beal looked it over and wasn't as bothered as me. He told me to sign it anyway. "This doesn't stop you from talking about the Rainbow Flag," he said. "You're Betsy Ross, for Christ's sake. The Rainbow Flag is about gay rights. Let the pharmacy talk about AIDS."

I wondered aloud if I hadn't been wrong in the first place by allowing the Rainbow Flag to get wrapped up in a corporate venture. "Maybe I've damaged the real beauty of the flag," I told Charley, "by making this big commercial deal out of it."

He reminded me that Stadtlanders didn't own the flag, that their brand name wasn't sewn on it. They only owned the mile-long version of the flag. He encouraged me again to sign the contract—and then disregard it.

"You mean, sign the contract and then break it?"

"Brilliant, isn't it?" Charley chuckled. "I'd say the fight over Fifth Avenue has only just begun. You have to do everything you can to make that the issue. Stop being a mouthpiece for that pathetic pharmacy and start protesting what's going down."

When I returned the signed contract, Stadtlanders responded with a conciliatory phone call, reassuring me this was just a formality for everyone's protection, and that we'd all pull together now as a team. I laughed to myself.

I packed up the sound system and went home. The flag was finished. The workshop, now filled with Stadtlanders executives, buzzed with an odd corporate energy, stiff and artificial. I asked them how the volunteer sign-up was going. It wasn't. They had less than half the people needed to carry the flag.

Diplomacy and compromise weren't my thing; I felt it was time to show Mayor Giuliani that our First Amendment rights couldn't be trampled. When all else fails, art is the ultimate weapon. A boiling rage inside dared me onward, leading me to my next creative scheme.

24

The Chiffon Rebellion

It was Flag Day, June 14, 1994. Moments before noon, Richard, Charley, Johann, Jude, and I assembled on the front steps of the New York Public Library, between the famous marble lions that guard the entrance to the building. A bright blue banner with pink lettering floated between the columns framing the doorway, reading BECOMING VISIBLE: THE LEGACY OF STONEWALL.

Inside, the press preview for this first-ever exhibition on the origins of the gay rights movement was about to conclude. In a few seconds, the television and newspaper reporters would exit this way. We didn't want the media to leave without a glimpse of our gay rights struggle in the present day.

When the first journalists emerged from the vestibule, on cue we unfurled an enormous Rainbow Flag I had sewn from translucent silk chiffon. It rippled in the brilliant Manhattan daylight. I had also sewn T-shirts into the corners of the flag, which we all put on. We were now part of the flag. Our Fruit of the Loom white T-shirts were splashed with red paint, reading CLASH in a slash-and-burn lettering style. It stood for "Civil Liberties Activists Shaping History"—the name of our ad hoc protest group. Jude had coined the acronym. We began chanting about our plan to march up Fifth Avenue on Pride Day in defiance of Mayor Giuliani.

When reporters saw Charley leading us in chants of outrage and protest, they plugged themselves back into their battery packs, focused their lenses, and went for the sound bite. Charley gave it to them straight and clear. "We are here on Flag Day with our Rainbow Flag to protest the mayor of New York's decision to not allow the gay pride parade on Fifth Avenue. We are here. We are queer. And we are going to march on Fifth Avenue—whether the mayor likes it or not."

Charley went on, warning Giuliani to stop playing the politics of confrontation. In just a few days, he declared, more than a million lesbians and gays would converge on the Big Apple to commemorate a riot that happened twenty-five years ago. If the city didn't cooperate with the community, he added ominously, then history would repeat itself.

We marched into the middle of Fifth Avenue and headed south. Our goal was to carry the flag, the symbol of our movement, to its birthplace, the Stonewall Inn, in the heart of Greenwich Village. Horns honked and cab drivers screamed obscenities while thousands of workers filled Fifth Avenue sidewalks on their lunch breaks, worsening the traffic jam. People wondered what it was all about. We handed out flyers.

We all held the Rainbow Flag high in the air, as surely as if it were a defiant fist. Richard Ferrara was up in front, holding the red corner, his strong arms thrusting the flag into the wind. Richard radiated power, and his wide Italian grin was like a child's, full of wonder and playful mischief. Jude Graham never stopped laughing. Her wild mane of big brunette hair was uncontrollable in the wind. Johann Moore was on the other corner, sewn into a swath of purple. A wisp of a man, who always wore a necktie during protests, he moved toward a television camera with his fist in the air, declaring, "Giuliani out of our way! Queers take Fifth on Gay Pride Day!"

Brian Griffin, a member of the street theater group Church Ladies for Choice, joined our march and began singing satirical parodies of hymns from the group's repertoire. He was an iconoclast for whom nothing was sacred, not even a Rainbow Flag. But he held tightly to a corner.

A few blocks away from the library, the press suddenly disappeared. Having gotten the story, they were rushing back to their newsrooms to meet their deadlines. All except Betsy Lenke, a longtime lefty activist and reporter for the equally lefty WBAI radio. She walked next to me, holding a microphone hooked into a small tape recorder.

"Why is the mayor doing this? What's his point?"

"The point is he can get away with it. The mayor can push the gay community around, as well as the Stonewall 25 organizers. The mayor is a big bully."

She asked about the tug-of-war over the flag's march route. I explained that while the flag belongs to Stadtlanders, the company was at the mercy of the mayor too, as he had determined the parade route. I explained that the flag she was seeing today did not belong to a corporate sponsor.

"Who does it belong to?" Betsy asked.

"To the people who love it," I declared.

"So, what about this big corporate sponsor? Is your vanity and ego as the creator being seduced by money?" Betsy's honesty surprised me.

"Maybe," I shrugged. "I'm the first to admit I'm a whore for art."

"Do you think there's still a future for gay liberation, or has its day passed?"

"There's always a future if you're willing to fight for it. We've forgotten how to mobilize. All our leaders suck up to political systems. They traded away a natural homosexual militancy for a facade of acceptance."

"So this flag here, what's the deal? Are you going to keep marching until they stop you?

"There aren't any cops around. Maybe we'll get all the way to the Stonewall bar."

Betsy asked if I knew that negotiations between Stonewall 25 organizers and the mayor's office were going on this very afternoon.

"The latest I heard is that the mayor's people want a list of all the speakers and performers. Can you imagine they want approval over everything, going so far as to tell us we can't invite Liza Minnelli?"

"Do you think the organizers will give it to them?"

"If they acquiesce to that kind of intimidation and censorship, I think it's over. Cowards!"

A policeman suddenly appeared and wanted to see our permit. We told him we didn't have one. He wanted to know if we had authorization. We told him we didn't need any. A squad car pulled up and the driver turned on his siren lights. We kept walking. The two policemen conferred, certain we were breaking some law. They called base for instructions. We kept walking, past the Empire State Building. Lesbian and gay faces appeared on the sidewalks, applauding us onward and shouting support. I thought it wouldn't be very long now before we were stopped and arrested.

Another police car tried to cut us off at an intersection, but we outran it. He moved behind us with his buddies in blue. I told a cop that he should consider escorting us. Let us march peacefully, I explained, and there wouldn't be any problem. I suddenly caught the reflection of the flag in the storefront windows. It was glorious. The homemade quality and giant scale reminded me of the first Rainbow Flag back in 1978. I shared a proud smile with Richard; we had all worked hard to create this moment. A few blocks in front of us, at Fifth Avenue and Fourteenth Street, I could see a barrier of blue uniforms and flashing red lights. We would not be having a drink at the Stonewall after all.

Meanwhile at city hall, two miles farther downtown, Franklin Fry and Pat Norman, national cochairs of the Stonewall 25 march, were meeting with one of the city's four deputy mayors. I could imagine Pat Norman, a San Francisco lesbian activist, looking at the deputy mayor and abruptly turning off her hip, black grandmotherly charm. She would play hardball, bringing up the possibility of a lawsuit if the city did not start cooperating.

I learned later that the deputy mayor said he didn't care about threats of a lawsuit. He insisted that the city had provided a "reasonable alternative" of a march in front of the United Nations. Clearly, the city had bowed to pressure from the Archdiocese of New York to make sure the flag would not parade past their citadel, St. Patrick's Cathedral. The deputy mayor threatened that all violators of the approved march route would be stopped. He warned that the city had a full police force of thirty thousand. As Pat and Franklin left the meeting, Franklin stopped, turned, and angrily sputtered, "You will not be able to stop us. Today is just the beginning."

By the time our CLASH protest reached Fifteenth Street, we saw about a hundred police officers putting on rubber gloves, plastic hand-cuffs tucked into their belts. A big sedan rolled up and a man in a suit got out of the backseat. He had an earphone on under a perfectly coiffed, blown-dry, salt-and-pepper hairpiece. He scanned the scene. People coming out of stores asked what was going on. One cop spoke through a squad car loudspeaker, announcing, "If you do not clear the street, you will be arrested." We kept walking.

The police started to move forward, so we all quickly sat down in traditional civil disobedience position and arranged the Rainbow Flag around ourselves, like nonviolent Buddhist monks. Johann, Richard, and I had agreed to risk arrest, while Charley, Jude, Brian, and the others would handle legal support while we were in jail. This would be my first New York City arrest. I was nervous. As they approached, the police walked on our flag in their black boots, leaving grimy prints. I looked at Richard and Johann and tried to absorb the Zen energy coming from their eyes. I wrapped myself tighter into the flag.

Hands were suddenly all over us. People were shouting. The big honcho in the suit said, "What the hell is that thing? Get it off of them." The cops finally realized the flag was sewn onto us. They cut it off with knives, ripping our shirts. It was the moment we had waited for. Charley became a deranged cheerleader, screaming that the police were desecrating the Rainbow Flag on Flag Day. He and Brian began to lead onlookers in shouts of "Shame! Shame!" More people pushed into the intersection. When they saw the gay flag being torn by police, they joined the shouting.

A big blond cop—who I noticed was cute—pulled my hands behind my back into plastic handcuffs. I was dragged to my feet. The cop sud-denly pulled me close and said, "You're under arrest—don't worry." I saw Richard also pulled to his feet. He wasn't resisting, this mountain of muscle in his red CLASH T-shirt. Johann was lying face-down in the prostrate position of priests when they take vows. Police picked him up by his skinny arms and legs. I was shoved into the backseat of a police cruiser and the blond cop slammed the door. Richard and Johann were pushed in from the other side. We were sweating profusely and my nose itched.

The blond cop got into the driver's seat and lowered the windows so we could breathe. He told us, "Don't worry. Once we book you, you'll be out in a couple of hours." I wondered why he was being so polite. His partner took the passenger seat.

The crowd was still yelling in support of us. The sedan pulled up beside us and Mr. Big screamed at the blond cop to get us out of there now or there was going to be trouble from onlookers. He looked at us and sneered. I called out to him, "Happy Flag Day!"

As the blond cop drove, his partner turned on the radio. Mick Jagger and the Rolling Stones were singing, "I can't get no satisfaction." We started singing along. The cops joined in, so that we were all grooving in unison to the line "But he can't be a man 'cause he doesn't smoke the same cigarettes as me." They wanted to know what we were protesting, so I told them all about the sordid political game going on down at the mayor's office. They couldn't believe that the annual pride march had been relocated.

We pulled up to the Pitt Street precinct on the Lower East Side. They handled bookings for Midtown Manhattan. We were led through the greasy doors of a waiting room down a wood-paneled hallway to cells. The blond cop was smiling, kind of bouncing on his feet. His eyes twinkled as he asked for our identification, taking our handcuffs off so we could hand our licenses to him. Richard gave me a nudge and insisted this guy was gay—that we had been hauled in by one of our own brothers.

We were then locked up—the only prisoners in a long row of dirty yellow cells. We were officially in jail. I looked into Richard's eyes and noticed he seemed a little sad, so I grabbed his hand.

We saw cops carry in the torn flag, remnants of the CLASH T-shirts dangling from its edges like scraps of red meat. The blond cop told the others to help him fold it up so he could fill out the inventory voucher. They grumbled but clumsily complied. "Hey, you guys," he asked, "remember how to fold a flag?" As he supervised the process, the blond suddenly interrupted the motions, saying, "No, you guys, you got it all wrong; the red stripe goes on the top."

The gay cop had given himself away! Johann was totally turned on. Richard and I were so delighted, we kissed each other. I tried to imagine what it must be like to be a gay cop. As the others placed the shredded flag in a clear plastic bag as evidence, the blond came over. He was carrying a sheet of paper and asked how much the flag was worth. I said, "Four thousand dollars," off the top of my head. Johann laughed, but I hushed him, adding, "You cannot buy a flag like this on Fifth Avenue for $10,000. I'm giving you the wholesale price."

"No way," the blond cop said, still smiling.

"OK, a thousand," I compromised. As he wrote down the figure on the document, I stressed that the flag material was chiffon. "C-h-i-f-f-o-n," I said, spelling it out for him.

When we looked over at him a while later, the blond cop held up the plastic bag with the flag, showing us that he was taking good care of it. Richard put his arm around my shoulder and gave me a quarterback hug, telling me, "It's not every day that a guy gets to arrest Betsy Ross."

"And on Flag Day at that," Johann added.

After signing the last of the police forms, we were freed. We walked through the front doors of Pitt Street station to find Charley and the others waiting for us. I ran to a pay phone and called Alan Klein, the gay publicist who was handling media for the day of the event.

As I told him the entire story, Alan was beside himself. "This might change everything!" he bubbled. "The good news is that Fifth Avenue and the dogfight going on are going to get a lot of attention now. The bad news is that your sponsors are going to shit bricks. Didn't you just sign a contract?"

Alan was right. When we arrived back at the workshop, the sweet pharmacy rep was hysterical. She wanted to know why I had done what I did. Just then, the workshop phone rang. It was another Stadtlanders person, equally pissed off.

"What are we going to do?" the woman on the phone asked, quite hostile.

"I don't care what you do," I shot back. "Go ahead and fire me if you think that's going to fix things."

An uncomfortable silence emanated from the receiver. In a calmer voice, she told me, "Well, I guess that we can't fire you." It was true; the march was twelve days away.

"I know it's hard for you to understand," I told her, gaining energy as I spoke, "but gay rights isn't in a test tube. It's alive and it's about fighting back. I've done my best to protect and enhance your presence in our community, but that's who I work for, not you." That speech touched off a firestorm of accusations and betrayed expectations that the Stadtlanders rep barked into my ear. When the woman was through venting, I calmly assured her that my plan for fighting back against the mayor's office was just beginning. I had no intention of stopping until the mile-long flag could be carried up Fifth Avenue.

"Well, don't ever use our name," she demanded.

"That's not a problem," I responded crisply, saying every word separately in a tone that suggested, *Fuck you.* The conversation was over.

The phone rang again. It was Ann Northrop from ACT UP. She explained that a group called Gay and Lesbian Americans was planning to file a lawsuit in federal court for the right to march up Fifth Avenue. She told me I had to be a part of it.

When I got off the phone with Ann, Richard walked over to me. He said calmly, "I'm quitting. The flag should go on Fifth Avenue. But the pharmacy is accepting First Avenue. As a matter of principle, I have to step aside."

Shock toppled me into a chair. "Resigning? Now?"

"I'll call you later," Richard said. He hugged everyone on his way out the door. "Don't worry, I can still volunteer," he added. As he got on his bike and rode off, I ran after him. He stopped and circled back so we could share a deep hug. I thanked Richard tearfully and vowed to do everything possible to be on Fifth Avenue with the mile-long flag.

Richard was walking away with integrity. But I felt like I was being swallowed up by my own monstrous creation, unable to let go.

25

A Day in Court,
a Night at Stonewall

The next week was spent in a haze of meetings and more meetings as Stonewall 25, ACT UP, and various radical factions all clamored to form a plan out of the general chaos of the coming Gay Pride weekend. On Thursday, June 23, a mere three days before the mile-long flag was scheduled to unfurl, clean shaven and well groomed, I made my way downtown to the federal courthouse. Crisp white jeans hugged my legs and an Aubrey Beardsley T-shirt covered my torso. Government buildings sizzled in the midafternoon heat. I waited patiently in the long line at security, then passed through the metal detectors and took an elevator up to the courtroom. It was unbearably hot, even with air-conditioning. I sat in the front row of long oak pews.

"Hear ye! Hear ye!" a bailiff declared, speaking like an eighteenth-century hallucination. "This court is now in session. All rise." The judge came in and sat behind a blond wood bench.

He would be presiding over a hearing about the city barring the mile-long flag from Fifth Avenue. But our case was listed at the bottom of the docket. It would be a while, so nobody else was there. Lawyers arrived in summer suits, carrying bulging briefcases. They sat at a table up in front. I moved back to the second row for a better view.

Michael Petrelis, the famed agitator, shuffled in. Michael had founded Gay and Lesbian Americans, the plaintiff in this case against Giuliani and the city. Big guns from the New York Civil Liberties Union had taken on the case. Michael was yawning and looked like he had just gotten up. He also seemed to be wearing dirty pajamas and shower thongs. I motioned for him to join me.

"I wanted some attention," Michael pouted, "but now you're here."

"Stonewall 25, Gay Games, your ridiculous flag," he continued. "The whole damn thing is so corporate, meaningless. You're just on a bunch of ego trips, aren't you, Blanche?" Michael added, camping in a Bette Davis voice.

"Don't fuck with me," I replied in perfect Joan Crawford style. "What are our chances here?"

"I have no idea, but there's been a lot of press calling and a couple of media vans outside."

A few others arrived—ACT UP's Ann Northrop entered in cutoff jeans and a tank top—but the public was far outnumbered by lawyers. In the stifling heat, even the judge took off his black robe and rolled up his shirtsleeves. Dress codes for days like this were thrown out in favor of cool survival. Well, not for everyone. The city's legal team arrived, all tailored to perfection. Hacks from the mayor's office took their reserved seats along the wall. It took some time, but the matter at hand was finally announced by the clerk.

From behind thick glasses, the judge gave a glance that instantly summoned the counsel from both sides to his chair. Try as we might, we couldn't hear what they were saying. But it seemed some kind of deal was being offered. After a few moments of muffled discussion, the judge banged his gavel and we all adjourned to the hall to hear what the city was offering. Ann, Michael, me, and a few others sat on the cool, polished marble floor in a circle like Indian chiefs. We listened to the city lawyers. But there was no compromise reached. So we returned to the courtroom. The case would proceed.

The judge heard the arguments presented by both sides. Whenever the city attorneys spoke, Michael, Ann, and the others made angry comments audibly. Our sweaty and unruly rabble seethed, glaring at the beasts on the other side of the wood railing. When a yuppie from the mayor's office insisted that New York City did not have enough police to staff two march routes, Michael responded with a loud "Liars!" that prompted the judge to bang his gavel and demand order.

"But they'll have enough police to arrest us—you can count on that," Ann whispered. She'd heard the city had assigned more police to Stonewall 25 than to any previous New York City Pride parade. Thousands of officers were looking forward to overtime.

The city suddenly was ready to make another offer, so we recessed a second time to the hall. A march might be allowed on half of Eighth Avenue. Again we refused. They had more compromises. All of Eighth Avenue, then half of Sixth Avenue. We refused both offers.

City lawyers huddled again and soon came back with one final offer: half of Fifth Avenue for the mile-long Rainbow Flag. If they would give us all of Eighth Avenue, we responded, then why not all of Fifth? Our answer was still no. City lawyers grumbled, calling us unreasonable. But we stood firm. When we reported back to the judge about our impasse, he decided that the matter would be given a full hearing the next day. Court was adjourned.

Friday morning, I dressed in high clone: a pair of white jeans and an Izod alligator shirt. We were now in a different courtroom, behind two massive oak doors adorned in gold-leaf lettering. Ornate wood paneling covered the walls and giant chandeliers dripped from a great height. The American flag, an old silk one, was a dominant feature in a terraced mahogany landscape of benches and risers. Above it all, the grand bench for the judge hovered—the throne of justice.

A bevy of lawyers entered with a flourish and walked up the center aisle. They were dwarfed in a room designed to hold hundreds. Michael Petrelis and Ann Northrop followed. We all went to our respective corners—the city lawyers on one side, our attorneys from the NYCLU on the other. The press box was full, and a small cluster of the public sat in the gallery.

The proceedings were conducted in muffled words. That is, until the chief of police declared that he would only support the plan of allowing the mile-long Rainbow Flag on First Avenue. The chamber erupted at this development. The judge banged his gavel and declared he would hand down a final ruling later that night. He also urged the city and Gay and Lesbian Americans to continue discussions about allowing a simultaneous protest march up Fifth Avenue, though a compromise seemed unlikely.

We were sure we'd been screwed. Ann Northrop was mad as hell. I walked out of the courthouse, feeling like a big apple had been shoved up my ass. A reporter asked me what we would do if the judge denied us a permit to march along Fifth Avenue. Exasperated, I told him we were going to surround St. Patrick's Cathedral and ram the Rainbow Flag through the front door.

Outraged, I headed uptown and donned a black sequined gown and the silver Streisand wig I had been saving for a special occasion. I jumped in a cab and headed to Tompkins Square Park for the first annual Drag March. By the time I arrived, a menagerie of outrageous drag queens and crazy costumed characters were gathering on the west side of the park.

Charley and Jude showed up as the crowd swelled. Suddenly, the immense group parted, revealing a drunken Judy Garland impersonator in a silver sequined shift, clutching a bottle of bourbon in one hand and a giant bottle of pills in the other. She prowled around in a circle, maniacally singing the Garland standard "Get Happy" while swigging the booze and tossing the pills at her face. Suddenly, she collapsed and lay dead on the ground. Solemnly, members of the Church Ladies for Choice lifted her on a bier and started the procession across town toward the West Village.

I unfurled a silver and purple banner I had made for the occasion and, clutching a silver high heel above my head, took my place at the front of the parade. As we headed along Ninth Street, an incredulous police escort flanked our growing throng. We sang and chanted until we reached the Stonewall on Christopher Street. There, hundreds of revelers welcomed us like conquering heroes. A contingent of half-naked Radical Faeries joined us inside for a drink. Later, Charley, Jude, and I headed to a Chelsea loft on Sixth Avenue, where the drag queens and faeries drummed deep into the night and we danced ourselves into exhaustion.

On Saturday morning, one day before Stonewall 25, I opened the *Times* to read that, as suspected, the judge had denied the Fifth Avenue permit, yet he also chastised the city for not being more flexible. The police stance was still the same: if any protestors headed for Fifth Avenue, officers would block traffic but could not guarantee that marchers wouldn't be arrested.

I felt depressed at the idea that Mayor Giuliani had won and contemplated packing my bags and leaving that day for San Francisco. But a major task awaited me at the flag workshop.

When I got there, about two hundred volunteers, including Charley and Richard, had already gathered. Our challenge was to move the mile-long flag up the stairs and into the yellow Ryder rental truck with molten chrome fenders, driven by my San Francisco friend Tom Taylor. Karen and Lucy from Stadtlanders came to supervise.

The process required perfect teamwork. I was barking instructions like a drill sergeant, explaining that all sections of the flag should be positioned with the tie sides up. I had devised an exact method for the load-up: the first layer of the fabric went on the truck bed front to back, then the next layer went in side to side, and so forth, until the entire seven thousand pounds were loaded. It was the only way to guarantee that the flag would come out of the truck the next day without tangles.

That morning, there was another, equally crucial task. Representatives from the *Guinness Book of World Records* had sent a document, asking us to confirm the mile-long length of the banner. That would ensure that the longest flag ever made would be included in the next edition of the book. The paper required a signature by both an attorney

From left to right: Gilbert, Jude Graham, Charley Beal, and Richard Ferrara after loading the three-and-a-half-ton Rainbow Flag into the rental truck.
Photo by Mick Hicks

and a member of the clergy. Matt Foreman, an LGBT attorney and a founder of Heritage of Pride, signed, followed by Richard's friend Father Bernard Lynch, a gay Irish Catholic missionary.

It took several hours to snake the flag up the stairs, out onto the street, and into the Ryder. Jude, Charley, and Richard joined me in the truck to pull in the yards and yards of rainbow fabric. The sun was beating down and we were all sweating ferociously in that stuffy metal box, so the guys took off their shirts. That made the process a little less backbreaking and a lot more sexy.

When the flag was finally loaded, I headed off to Number 9. Alice was waiting on the third floor with Johann, and they handed me a big fat joint.

"ACT UP and a few other groups are going ahead with their illegal march up Fifth Avenue despite the police," Alice explained. "They're still smarting over the treatment they got in March on the Brooklyn Bridge. They're talking about fighting back this time."

We discussed what I should do. Should I hijack the flag? I knew Tom Taylor would be game, but Stadtlanders would have me arrested. We cracked open a couple of beers and smoked another joint as an endless stream of people came over, hungry for the latest news on the march.

Later that evening, I headed out to see if I could find Ann Northrop to learn the details of what ACT UP was really planning. But my search was in vain; Ann had joined tens of thousands of lesbians for a giant Dyke March through the Village. Exhausted, I dragged myself home and decided to call my friends back in San Francisco with an update. But no one was home at that hour in California.

By 10:00 PM, I was alone in bed, listening to the sound of a million people outside. Saturday soon became Sunday. It was one o'clock in the morning and I knew I wasn't going to sleep. So I threw on some clothes and headed for the door. As I turned the brass knob, I found Jude Graham on the other side. "Going out," she said. It wasn't a question. She was also wide awake. "Whaddya say we head down to the Stonewall for a drink," she offered. It was her treat.

Jude held my hand and we walked over to Eighth Avenue. When we got to the flag workshop, Adrian Mason, a friend who had helped with folding the flag, was just coming around the corner. We invited him to join us for a drink. We decided to take a couple of large remnant sections from the mile-long Rainbow Flag to the Stonewall for a sneak preview. My ego needed a boost.

"People will love this," Adrian said. "It will be like a magical dance when they get their hands on it." He and Jude carefully folded up the pieces and put them in garbage bags for a cab trip down Seventh Avenue to Christopher Street.

When we piled out, Christopher Street was packed elbow to elbow with people drumming and dancing. Lesbian and gay couples were making out on the iron benches in the little park across the street. This was what we lived for: a moment to be free and proud, celebrating our love. In front of the Stonewall, we set our cargo on the pavement in the glow of the red neon sign in the window. I could hear RuPaul's "House of Love" blasting from inside the bar. The three of us each opened a bag and started pulling fabric out of it. Color was flying in every direction.

Jude and Adrian began shouting for everyone to join in the process and scores of hands were suddenly grabbing cloth in streaks of motion. The multitude lifted the flag pieces high into the air. The word went out and more people began gathering. The crowd steadily swelled until it reached Seventh Avenue. Cops began to take notice, drawn by the size of the gathering.

We watched the crowd play tug-of-war with the banner pieces. At least they couldn't tear them apart. I was satisfied our sewing would hold up. Everyone danced under the colors, raising and lowering them. The rapid movement of the cloth stirred a current of handmade wind that cooled us like air-conditioning. On such a warm night it was a sensual delight.

We were in front of the symbolic birthplace of the modern lesbian and gay rights movement. My mind went back to 1969, twenty-five years before, when angry drag queens had battled the police. And tonight I saw a thin line of blue uniforms trying to corral a few celebrants who had decided to hold an impromptu protest by sitting in the middle of Seventh Avenue. It was still the same: cops versus queers. The authority of the state against the will of the people. Stonewall had been a riot. Many felt another insurrection was the only real way to convey the significance of Stonewall 25 to a new generation.

I realized that most people on the street this evening didn't know that the day before, in federal court, the police had tried to sabotage this year's march, to push it out of sight. *Fuck the city*, I thought, *We're going to do what we want.* Power is always taken, never given. I thought of the chant Cleve and I loved: "The people united will never be defeated." Truth, courage, and love are the seeds of revolution. Tonight we savored the legacy of our predecessors, standing before the Stonewall Inn.

The showdown about our access to Fifth Avenue was only a few hours away. Even if the authorities backed off and let the alternative march proceed unchallenged, I felt city hall had won. We had scared

The approved and unapproved parade routes for Stonewall 25. *Map design by Chris Erichsen*

them with our numbers and rhetoric, but they had beaten us down in court. Giuliani had succeeded in controlling gay community organizers with an iron fist. Uptown at St. Patrick's Cathedral, I heard, they were already setting up barricades.

It was almost 3:00 AM Sunday morning. The streets were still electrified with partiers. We had lost Adrian long ago, when he went traipsing off with a piece of the flag. Jude and I never got around to having a drink inside the Stonewall. She took hold of my hand and led me home. She said it was important to lie down, blood flowing toward the brain, for a rest. We needed it. We took off our clothes and turned the fan on high. But I couldn't help but go over the strategy for the morning one more time.

I suddenly had a solution to the stalemate. A strategy for revolt. One pair of scissors could change the whole dynamic. When the First Avenue parade ended, I would cut the mile-long Rainbow Flag in several pieces. A few pieces would be secretly smuggled to Fifth Avenue and we would march them defiantly in front of St. Patrick's Cathedral.

Jude loved my idea. It was four o'clock in the morning, but she got on the phone to recruit friends to help us carry out our secret eleventh-hour plan.

26

A Magician, a Mile of Scarf, and a Pair of Scissors

My eyes were closed but I was awake. A slow dawn meandered into our apartment, first striking our leopard skin pillows. Jude and I snuggled for another moment. Then we greeted the morning with the blessing of being two dear friends, simultaneously saying, "I love you."

What to wear on a day that was either going to be a fiasco or a triumph? At the last moment, I decided on the silver sequined gown, even though I had already worn it sensationally at the Gay Games opening ceremonies a few days earlier at Columbia University's Wien Stadium. Jude grabbed a bottle of water from the fridge. I shoved the gown into a yellow Tower Records shopping bag. We ran down the tiny twisted staircase and out the front door and hailed a cab, telling the driver we were heading to First Avenue and Thirty-Sixth Street.

Tom Taylor was waiting by the flag-filled Ryder truck. He and I confabbed a moment about exactly where to place the banner in the street. When we opened the doors to the truck, I was relieved to see that the flag had remained in place, down to its precise folds. Tom took charge of the vehicle, while Jude and I headed off to find the sound people.

One of them, Mike Lefleur, walked up, carrying a strange-looking bullhorn wrapped around his shoulder. He told me that he hated the thing and would prefer not to be saddled with it as we walked. I lowered my voice and told him there had been a change of plans for Raise the Rainbow. He would have a different assignment this afternoon. I pulled out a pair of scissors from my shopping bag and explained quietly.

Mike's eyes grew wide with excitement. But then he frowned and began muttering. "What happens when these people see you cutting it? They might think you're some crazy attacking it and try to stop you. Have you considered there could be a panic? What about the pharmacy? Do they know you're going to cut it up?" I responded to every objection, until Mike finally calmed down.

My friend Robbie Tucker arrived, carrying a shopping bag full of orange juice and baked goods. She warned us that if we got hungry, there wasn't a damn thing in Central Park but hot dogs. She stuffed bagels and croissants into our hands. I filled her in on the mission.

"Yeah, well, that will just wreck the cops," Robbie said, beaming. "Just go on and rub it in their faces."

Charley turned up with an old comrade of his, Mary Hanerfeld. We discussed the mechanics of our surprise revolt. When we arrived with the mile-long flag at Fifty-Sixth Street, people would start folding it up. While everyone was still focused on the back end of the flag, I would be at the front end, cutting several sections. Everyone would grab a section, fold it up, and head to Fifth Avenue, where we would regroup in front of the New York Public Library to join the illegal march. In case cops intercepted a couple of us and confiscated our flag segments, we would all take different routes to Fifth. That would increase the probability of success. Charley also explained the logistics for the helicopter photo ops, so that our insurrection would be documented even if it was cut short.

Mary suddenly hissed, "They're coming," and gestured with her head. We looked up to see the Stadtlanders reps, Lucy and Karen, approaching with their signature frozen smiles.

From behind, I heard the voice of my publicist, Alan Klein. He grabbed me by both arms and pushed me away from the sponsors and straight toward a reporter from ABC's *Good Morning America.* "If you fuck this up," he whispered, only half joking, "I will kill you."

"We're counting on you," was all Karen could say before the camera lights came up and they began filming.

After a smooth interview, I directed my volunteers to open up about sixty feet of the flag for a perfect TV visual. Then I headed over to the portable stage that Dana Beal's friend Alan Thompson had parked nearby. It was a refurbished Peterbilt flatbed truck the Yippies used at all their protest rallies. On the back was a large sound system playing Etta James and the Rolling Stones. Alan reached down and gave me his hand, pulling me up onto the stage.

I saw thousands of eyes focused on the fabulous Rainbow Flag billowing up toward Thirty-Seventh Street. Elevated, I could see a long way up First Avenue. The United Nations Building was obscured by a wall of twenty-five-story smokestacks at a Con Ed plant just a couple of blocks away. Further up, where the roadway divided at Forty-Second

Gilbert and a volunteer on the Raise the Rainbow stage, June 26, 1994. *Photo by Charley Beal*

Street, a blue blur of police were eating donuts around a tiny platform that had been set up for the Stonewall 25 committee.

Slowly, more and more people filled the vacant space. After a cup of coffee and a clandestine toke, I relaxed. More volunteers showed up. Everywhere you saw the Rainbow Flag—on white T-shirts, on hats, on scarves, on every conceivable garment and accessory, much of it home-made. I always loved that stuff.

Roberta Achtenberg arrived. My longtime ally from my San Francisco days was now assistant secretary at the Department of Housing and Urban Development. With her was Joe van Es–Ballesteros, who had worked with Cleve and me on Pink Saturday. He had come to New York just to help me out. But Cleve would not be here; he had stayed home in California, too ill to travel, bitterly disgusted, and hating me.

I noticed Roberta was wearing a garden smock in a tasteful safari print. It made me recall how she had battled with Senator Jesse Helms at her confirmation hearings, remaining dignified while he attacked her. Helms had called her "mean" and "not your garden-variety lesbian." It was amazing that she still had a sense of humor after she had been trashed coast to coast.

When Roberta climbed up onto the stage with me, I asked her if these huge gatherings meant anything anymore. I confessed that I felt Stonewall 25 was ultimately a commercial for marketing and merchandising the movement, an advertisement of power rather than an act of empowerment. I told her how angry I was that the community had sold out to Mayor Giuliani on the parade route, and how weak he made us look.

"But we're here and your flag is here," Roberta said. "Isn't that what really matters? Sure, it would have been better on Fifth Avenue, but it's still a tremendous success. You should be proud, Gilbert." She touched my arm and looked deeply into my eyes. I felt a lump in my throat. Tears welled up. I heaved a sigh that released some of the tension.

Wiping the tears away, I thought about Richard Ferrara. I was in love with him and it was ruining our friendship. I had promised to meet him for the guerrilla action in front of the library on Fifth Avenue.

But he would not join us to unfurl the Rainbow Flag on First Avenue. I wondered if we would find each other in the throngs on Fifth. For a moment, I balanced faith and rage. I thought to myself, *I'm always holding the end of the rainbow on the outside, knowing inside there's only darkness.*

I realized Roberta still had a hold of my arm as we both crossed to a microphone. She began introducing me, but I wasn't listening. A thousand voices echoed through my mind, as I recalled the supporters and opponents who had passed through my life during the last year while I was working on the flag. Suddenly, I was shaken from my thoughts by great roars from the thousands now assembled. I looked out and saw the reason for their excitement: Tom Taylor had just opened up a whole block-long section of the Rainbow Flag.

"Good morning, New York City!" I thundered out in my best Robin Williams imitation. "This is not brain surgery, and you won't need a manual." What I said after that, I don't even recall, but I luckily remembered a list of thank-yous, ending with a corny cheer, "Do it! Let's raise the rainbow."

A huge wave of people surged forward, each grabbing on to an edge of the flag.

We jumped down off the stage and ran up to the front, where the Big Apple Corps, the city's gay marching band, was in formation. Each uniformed member wore a bright rainbow sash. The director gave me a high five, then cued the musicians so the *rat-a-tat* of snare drums began. The drum major raised a baton while trumpets blasted the opening bars of "New York, New York." I could feel my hair electrified.

I watched a contingent of Stadtlanders people stepping off behind a blue banner. The orange-handled Fiskars scissors burned in my pocket. I grabbed on to the front of the flag and pulled Roberta and Joe in close with me. After a block of smooth travel, I let go and started running back underneath it, encouraging people to lift it high into the air. I was laughing and dancing under the tall billows in the moving, silken swells of the fabric. I looked down. The sun shining through the flag projected an intense, glittering light on the street. I was walking on diamonds.

I ran wildly back to where the flag was still emerging from the rear of the truck, a geyser of fabric shooting up the street. Tom Taylor was inside, feeding out the carefully coiled multicolored hose to a huge assembly line of coordinated volunteers. Charley, Jude, and Mike were on one side, untying thousands of bows. I jumped in on the opposite side with Robbie and Phill Leach and his boyfriend Warren, friends of Richard's who had come for the parade from London. Together we handed the fabric out to the hundreds of people queued up.

The flag made a whooshing sound like water from a spring. Faster and faster it gushed through our hands. In seconds, we had lost control. The string ties started popping off with a strange embryonic sound. *Poppity-pop, poppity-pop.* We just let it happen. As the flag unfurled, the force of the expanding mass of fabric took incredible strength to grasp. More and more people joined hands to spread the Rainbow Flag wider.

The front of the flag soon disappeared over the top of the rise at Forty-Second Street. I waited a few moments until I knew the lead edge was a quarter mile out and everyone along each side could feel the full force of wind, the weight, and the enormous mass. It was inspiring— and intimidating.

Helicopters crisscrossed high above. In one of them was our official photographer, Mick Hicks. I hoped he was getting good shots.

The mile-long Rainbow Flag was now performing perfectly. Once every few minutes, the wind would lift parts of it high into the air. Nylon swirled away from our hands, flowing out past the horizon. I could hear cheers and roars of amazement echoing up and down the avenue. The applause was deafening.

I looked back downtown, seeing thousands more people queued up, moving slowly toward us, ready to join the thousands already carrying the flag. In that moment, the fears I had carried around for months about having enough volunteers finally evaporated. It had happened. We had built it, and they had come. I took off my official T-shirt and slipped on the silver sequined gown. Dramatic and gorgeous, it slithered over my skin. As the hem tumbled to the asphalt, I raised my arms high in triumph. The screams of appreciation left no doubt in my mind that I was in charge. This was the moment to perform. I walked toward the very back of the procession, making sure everyone, to the last person, saw me in the dazzling regalia. I took my bows and started dancing my way uptown under the flag.

Block by block, I was flying, spinning and hurtling past each person carrying the flag. My feet barely touched the ground as I was lifted by the light in everybody's eyes. Waving to them all in triumph, my hand suddenly began shaking. I was about to set my secret mission into operation.

I passed the crest of Forty-Second Street, then downhill to Forty-Sixth Street, where they fly the flags of different countries in front of the United Nations Building. Everywhere I looked, there were marchers, spectators, and throngs of cops.

I kept running until I made my way up to the front of the flag at Fifty-Sixth Street, then pulled out my Fiskars. I had finally come to the climax of the performance: a magician, a mile of scarf, and a pair of scissors.

A walkie-talkie crackled, announcing that the front of the flag had reached Fifty-Seventh Street. I looked as far as I could in both directions at my creation. My skull absorbed the illusion of this Rainbow Flag laid out in horizontal infinity, painted on vertical Manhattan. It had taken a year of work—and the artistic and political triumph would last only this brief moment. I got the attention of everyone in the immediate area around me, flashing my Fiskars, and then announced what was about to happen.

The summer sun touched deep inside of me. I felt relaxed and natural. My left fingers held the purple hem firmly. My right thumb and index finger squeezed the metal blades together. One chop through the triple-thickness seam, then slice and run. When I looked up, I was moving through the middle of the flag, cutting a swath across the avenue.

There were yelps of alarm and cries of confusion from marchers. But I loudly assured everyone this was all part of the plan. I would cut it, then move back a dozen yards and then cut it again. Out of a teary corner of my eye, I glimpsed Charley shouldering away a huge bundle.

Robbie grabbed the next one, then Jude and Adrian another. I heard all my strategically stationed conspirators shouting instructions, taking command amid the confusion. They were pushing colors this way and that way, quickly and neatly folding the pieces up by the seams.

The operation was over in less than a minute. Now, ten big pieces of the flag were on their way to Fifth Avenue.

All the side streets were full of cops, endless battalions. NYPD helicopters still buzzed overhead. With Phill and Warren, we grabbed the last two pieces and raced back down to Thirty-Fifth Street, where there were fewer cops. Joined by Mike, we heaved our bundles toward the barricades at Second Avenue. I created a diversion by loudly shouting instructions about loading the flag into a truck around the corner. There wasn't one. The officers just looked at us blankly. The bluff worked. We just kept going.

In a New York minute, we were in a cab and telling the driver to step on it. Down to the Twenties, right, then right again on Madison Avenue, heading uptown to Fortieth Street and Fifth Avenue. When we arrived at the New York Public Library, the cabbie popped the trunk and we seized the twisted mass of fabric with all our might. The heavy load felt good. We felt strong. The four of us reached the center of Fifth Avenue, where the lines of the crosswalks intersected with the traditional lavender stripe painted down Fifth every June, an annual ritual that took place the night before the parade.

The alternative Stonewall 25 march had busted out of Greenwich Village an hour before. A quarter of a million people were making their way up Fifth Avenue in defiance of the city, the mayor, and the cops. As they approached the library, it felt like a homecoming. We could see large ACT UP placards carried high above the crowd. Our tiny group was swept up in the human current.

The first flag section was lifted up and opened wide. We carried the Rainbow Flag past the library. This one was bigger than the one we were arrested with only two weeks before. On the steps, a man in a huge tulle ball gown twirled under the Becoming Visible exhibition banner. I leaped up the stairs and we took a couple of turns together. The sun almost set my dress on fire, every sequin exploding with star energy. I never felt more fabulous—and I was wearing such sensible shoes.

I wiped away the perspiration and looked uptown toward Rockefeller Center and St. Patrick's Cathedral, eight blocks north. I scanned the avenue for signs of Richard. You could see his bright smile a block away. He was so handsome in white cutoffs and shirtless. We finally found each other.

"I can't believe you're only twenty minutes late," Richard marveled. "This is amazing." We took pictures and sprayed each other with water. We had accomplished our revolt. It was a sweet moment.

Charley had everything arranged perfectly. As each courier rendezvoused, each of the ten flag pieces was meticulously unfolded—enough to cover two city blocks of Fifth Avenue. We moved into position at the southern corner of St. Patrick's Cathedral. I licked my lips in anticipation.

God's temple was blockaded with row after row of wooden barricades. An elaborate security detail completely sealed off the church from the public. High up in the spires, sharpshooters were poised. Out on the street, the boys in blue stood shoulder to shoulder, holding nightsticks, their faces masked behind greasy plastic shields. I caught the eye of one man in uniform sporting the biggest amount of gold braid and called out, "What, no barbed wire?"

The territorial imperative was all for show; they weren't about to do anything.

A volley of protestor voices screamed toward the locked doors. You could hear it echo deeply in the gothic bowels of the granite citadel. The cardinal would have to cover his ears—or else he would hear. The words were ringing with such force, they burned into my soul. For a second, I imagined the pretentious palace of faith crumbling into a subterranean hell.

"You can't stop us and you can't stop our flag!" a new voice declared, full of Jericho. I tried to see who was shattering the walls with righteous protest, but was blinded by sunlight. I suddenly realized it was Charley.

A contingent of Radical Faeries were taking off their clothes in protest, standing stark naked in front of the cathedral. They kissed passionately, their provocative sexual excitement nearly melting the asphalt. Photographers closed in. The great crowd began to chant, "Fuck you! Fuck you!" in unison. That gave way to just "Fuck! Fuck! Fuck!" in cathartic explosions that blasted across the patriarchal edifice. The police were itching to arrest them, but the thin blue line stayed in formation.

We walked on defiantly, carrying the rippling flag sections. It was another nine blocks to Central Park. When we came to the huge open field known as the Great Lawn, we lifted the flags triumphantly high into the air and saluted our people. The rainbow banners floated above our heads all the way to the foot of the event stage.

Our special mission team found a place behind a line of media trucks and finally collapsed, exhilarated by what we had accomplished. We rested on our soft heap of color, holding each other. I closed my eyes and soon lost consciousness.

I was awakened by an attractive African American woman in blue jeans asking for an interview. Barbara Wood of NY1, the New York City twenty-four-hour cable news channel, explained that she knew everything about the Rainbow Flag—even about the secret plan to go from the United Nations to Fifth Avenue. She had covered our Fifth Avenue stealth mission live. I asked Richard to come with me and followed her. Wood climbed a shiny ladder on the back of NY1's white media van with a satellite dish, then reached down a hand and invited us to join her.

I hitched up my dress and tucked it into my shorts and began maneuvering up the platform, tangled in chiffon and sequins. Richard gracefully followed. We wrapped our arms around each other, taking in the spectacle. As we looked out over a huge gathering from atop the TV truck, someone on the stage recognized me and called out my name. The massive crowd roared its approval and it felt like we were being sprayed with champagne.

Gilbert and Richard celebrate the success of their Stonewall 25 guerrilla action on top of a TV news van in Central Park. *Photo by Charley Beal*

At that moment of artistic triumph, I was proud to be arm in arm with Richard Ferrara, the man I had fallen in love with during this project. Our love for each other transcended any words. The Rainbow Flag was all about the soul power radiating from our beautiful bodies—not just him and me, but all one million of us this afternoon, marking the twenty-fifth anniversary of the Stonewall riots with a new act of pure rebellion to support the Rainbow Flag.

Richard and I lingered a few moments on top of New York City. Only a few feet off the ground, we felt as if we had climbed the highest mountain together. On the far horizon, the famous silver skyscrapers of Central Park South beamed above the multitudes. We touched, forever blood brothers.

The afternoon drifted under the lazy shade. Charley and I left early to catch the national news. Somehow, we got a cab in front of the Metropolitan Museum of Art and made it to his West Village apartment just in time. We watched the final product, our triumph, come to life on TV. ABC News opened with aerial footage showing the Rainbow Flags passing St. Patrick's Cathedral and dissolved to the shot of the mile-long flag in front of the United Nations. The Rainbow Flag was the lead news on every channel. It worked exactly as Charley and I had engineered, exceeding all expectations. The air-conditioning was on and we stripped down to cool off, while changing the channels. Zap, zap, zap.

"Well, you've really started something now," Charley said. "This is just the beginning of the Rainbow Flag. Today, the butterfly left the cocoon."

Later, I walked home feeling elated. But there was still one final task. I sat on my apartment bed and called Cleve in California. I owed him a thank-you. I wanted my conscience to be clear. My fingers trembled a little, pushing the buttons. After a few rings, he answered. All my emotions became twisted in my throat, but I managed to tell him, "I just wanted to say thanks a million. It was great."

Cleve didn't say anything except a hostile final good-bye.

I expected it. But I had done my part, making a courtesy call that closed the book on our New York City love-hate experience. I squeezed the last drop of love from that friendship. I almost felt a bloody taste in my mouth when I hung up the phone. For me, the Stonewall 25 experience was magical and inspirational. For Cleve, it was ugly and confrontational. I had put my art up against his politics and it had killed our friendship.

In the evening, I met up with Richard on the West Village piers and watched the traditional fireworks over the Hudson. Glittering explosions illuminated the river to the music of Gershwin's "Rhapsody in Blue." Resting in the arms of my beloved friend, I began to accept that this was the end of a long journey.

On the way home, we ran into Michael Petrelis sitting in Sheridan Square. When he saw us, he began waving the early morning edition of the *New York Times*, screaming "Betsy Ross, media queen!" On the front page was a massive photo of the Rainbow Flag—five columns wide and above the fold.

I took a deep breath and turned to Richard. I had been thinking about this moment all day. I looked directly into his handsome face and asked if he would come home and spend this special night with me. Richard paused. He shook his head sadly, and claimed that it was late and that he had to get home. He got on his bike, gave me a hard hug and a quick kiss, then rode off in the moonlight. I felt my heart break, but I prayed that Richard would make it home safely and that our friendship would last.

When the party's over and all the balloons have popped, New York is a bittersweet place to be. Nursing an inner ache, I watched night become dawn. Then I ambled home alone and slept, releasing in dreams all the tumultuous emotions of the day.

In the morning, the Rainbow Flag was emblazoned across the front page of every major newspaper—in New York City, across America, and across the world. I went around to every newsstand, buying up every copy I could find, my arms filling with newsprint as if I were carrying a colorful bouquet. At a classy art supply store on Fifth Avenue, I bought two big black leather portfolios. Over the next couple of days, I clipped all the best news photos and made expensive color copies. In the cool of evening, I created identical scrapbooks chronicling the victory of Stonewall 25; one for myself and the other for Richard.

Bob Dylan sang, "There's no success like failure, and that failure's no success at all." Cleve was the one who had it all, a man who could move mountains. He'd given me an opportunity to do the same, and I'd done everything right. But the truth was more complicated. On the surface, Stonewall 25 was a success. But underneath, there were tattered recriminations and a mortally wounded friendship. However, I clung to the vain hope that someday Cleve and I would meet together in a place where more forgiving pastures begin.

The folks at Stadtlanders couldn't get rid of me fast enough. I was just the seamstress and the wedding was over. The big dance between gay rights and corporate America fizzled out as fast as the fireworks over Manhattan. In the end, Stadtlanders left the party and took the mile-long, legendary Rainbow Flag with them. To the victor, the spoils. Unbeknownst to them, I had arranged for the ten rogue Fifth Avenue pieces to be given to delegations from various countries around the world. A year later, those flags would fly in Cuba, London, China, Brazil, and elsewhere. The project that had started in a loft in San Francisco sixteen years earlier would finally become a globally recognized icon.

I saw Richard and Charley one last time for breakfast at the Bus Stop, our favorite diner in the West Village. Richard acted as if our previous farewell on Pride night had never happened. He listened as I yammered and processed the chaotic events of the last few months—Stadtlanders, Cleve, Flag Day, Stonewall 25, Giuliani, St. Patrick's—and gave me a big shoulder to lean on. He also had advice for the future: I should focus on creating things for myself, whether it was painting or writing. Then Richard hugged me tightly—as a friend and comrade. Charley Beal gave me a key to his Village apartment for my next return visit.

There's an old saying, "When you're not in New York, you're just camping out." I threw my two bags in the trunk, and my taxi headed for the airport. En route, just to make conversation, the cab driver asked me where I lived.

I didn't have an answer.

On board the plane, I allowed the force of the jet engines to push me back into my seat. The Manhattan that had been home for almost a year vanished in the blue sky. San Francisco awaited me at the other end of the arc.

I think of my life's journey like a rainbow, only lasting a little while but connected to the Almighty. In the Bible, God says to Noah, "I do set my bow in the cloud, and it shall be for a token of a covenant between me and the earth." How many rainbows do we experience in a lifetime?

As the plane climbed higher, I looked forward to creating that next Rainbow Flag.

27

The Hatchet Is Buried

In December 2000, the day after the Supreme Court put George W. Bush in office, Cleve called me up in Los Angeles. We hadn't really spoken since the flag workshop debacle in New York. It had been six bitter years. Our time as estranged brothers had been tough on all our mutual friends, forcing them to walk a tightrope between us.

"I heard you're leaving the country," Cleve said, even before saying hello.

"I'm done here," I said, making it up. "London, I think."

"Don't go," he said, sounding sincere, friendly. "You should stay and fight."

"The fight is over in the US," I said coolly. "There's more important stuff elsewhere."

"London?" he sneered. "It's the same. You should stay. We need you." Cleve paused. "Well, I need you and I miss you." He waited a moment. "We should be friends."

Balancing the weight of his words on my emotions, I warbled, "And I miss you too, Cleve."

"You never called." There was that Cleve pettiness again, but his tone was measured.

"I called."

A beat of silence filled the void between us. We both lit up cigarettes.

215

"You know we need to get over this thing between us," Cleve said, getting right to the point. "I think we should get together and talk about it."

I was speechless. Cleve never talked like this. He was making me nervous. I wanted to agree to a meeting just to humor him and then hang up.

"No, I mean it," Cleve said. "I have some things to say to you and you have things to say to me. You should come over and visit me. We can work it out." He paused again. "I really love you."

It was a miracle. As I bit my lip, a few precious, cleansing teardrops fell from my eyes. I accepted his invitation.

I took a Greyhound from Los Angeles to Palm Springs, where Cleve had relocated in 1994. Living on the Russian River had almost killed him. Quoting Ella Fitzgerald, Cleve liked to sing, "Hate California, it's cold and it's damp." So he moved south, somehow combining his meager salary from the NAMES Project AIDS Memorial Quilt and the money he got for his memoir *Stitching a Revolution* into a down payment on a small house. I remembered how years ago at the dinner table, Cleve had described the ideal home and I had drawn his fantasy. We were amateur architects then, dreaming on graph paper.

Cleve picked me up at the little bus stop in the same car he always had, a tiny blue Honda two-door—now covered in desert dust. I laughed in seeing it, amused how everyone thought we were both so rich and famous from our activism. For someone with AIDS, he looked healthy and tan.

"You old queen," he teased as we embraced.

"Old as fuck!" I agreed, kissing him on both cheeks. "You're still handsome."

"You're such a liar, and ya always were, Blanche." For a minute, I felt we were back to our Bette Davis and Joan Crawford rivalry. But it was just camp. Cleve put my bag in the trunk and turned to me. "I'm really glad you came."

Cleve said he would make dinner, so we stopped at a grocery store for salmon and white wine. I went for small talk, mentioning that I heard Cleve had installed a pool. He gushed about it. "I blew all the money from the book on it! Wait till you see it. Natural Arizona sand-stone everywhere, and a Jacuzzi."

We pulled into the driveway of his '50s white tract house with a tall hedge and low brick wall surrounding the yard. He led the way into the living room, filled with his old, worn furniture. But the dining room had a new mission-style oak table and chairs. A big window overlooked the pool. Cleve made Cape Cod cocktails in plastic tumblers. After a quick tour of the seven pastel-colored rooms with low white ceilings, I unpacked in the celery-green guest room. I changed into an orange Speedo—a scary move at my age and girth.

"You got fat," Cleve said flatly.

"Fat and old. I look nothing like I used to. My ballroom days are over. But you look really good," I said, poking his belly. "Good and fat."

"Not as old and fat as you!" Cleve said, and I felt the tension between us loosen up. On the patio, the temperature was 110 degrees. My feet burned when they touched the sandstone. "Get in the water, girl, or you'll die!" Cleve said, hosing down the hot pavement, which turned a deep pink.

I dove in, headfirst. It was heaven.

Cleve jumped in and made a big splash deliberately. We climbed on matching turquoise pool rafts, drifting in the scorching sun, and sipped our vodka cranberry cocktails.

"You know, you really hurt me in New York," Cleve began abruptly. The small talk was over. Time to discuss matters, seriously, intimately. "But I forgive you." I recognized the Cleve tone that indicated he didn't completely forgive me. "You wrecked the pharmacy," he continued. "You used me. And then when I got sick, you ditched me, and I was very hurt by that."

It was a stinging scold. I thought about challenging his accusation and defending myself. But I suddenly changed my mind and said simply, "I'm sorry for the way I treated you. It wasn't fair." My apology hung in the air.

"You called me a megalomaniac to a reporter when my book came out, and that was very mean." Cleve wagged his finger at me. "And you of all people saying such a thing? That's the pot calling the kettle black."

I tried to lighten the mood. "It was meant as a compliment, one peer to another." I took a sip of my drink, bracing for his reply.

"It wasn't funny." He gave me the evil eye of disapproval. The comment in print had made him angrier than our clash of egos in New York.

"I'm sorry you took it the wrong way."

"Well, now I forgive you," Cleve said with full authority. This time I could tell he meant it. The edict welcomed back the banished.

And just like that we were friends again. Reconciliation.

The sun disappeared behind the mountain and a long lavender shadow cooled the still water reflecting the sky. We dried off with the blue beach towels I had brought as a gift. We gave each other updates on old friends and gossiped about them.

In the kitchen, Cleve was all business, slicing and dicing, making a special sauce from red peppers. We talked politics as I thumbed through his music collection. He had a lot of CDs, but also old LPs in their original album jackets. He waved me away and put on some African disco drum record. We started dancing.

"I met Nelson Mandela," he bragged, eyes sparkling, talking about running into the great man in a hallway in South Africa. "It was the most amazing thing ever!"

"Better than Clinton?" I teased.

"Oh, Bill and Hillary, that was something!" Cleve flashed a mischievous smile. "I think he's got a big one."

"Really? He is tall, but Mandela—better than Elizabeth Taylor?"

"Way better."

"Impossible," I scoffed.

As the tribal music ended, I asked if he had any Rolling Stones.

"No Rolling Stones and no Barbra Streisand ever!" Cleve declared proudly. "It's the twenty-first century." He put on U2.

We continued to talk of our current political situation, now that Bush had the White House. "Clinton fucked it up with a stupid blow job," he said.

"Yeah, but here we are. It's the end of democracy."

"We have to fight back. We can't just leave." I felt like Cleve was convincing himself more than me.

We talked about living as expatriates in another country. Or whether to stay and fight back. I suggested, half joking, taking up guns.

"Love power!" Cleve insisted, playfully strangling me. "You're so negative!" We danced to Marvin Gaye's LP *What's Going On.*

"Do everything you can," Cleve said, "and remember it was all my idea." There was a truth in there somewhere; I did owe Cleve a great deal.

Cleve set the table with tropical place mats, matching cloth napkins, two china plates, two wine glasses, and nice silverware. Candles were lit. Brazilian jazz music set the mood. We had Caesar salad and broiled salmon. I had seconds.

"You like it in New York?" he asked while we cleared the dishes. "Everyone says you're a superstar there."

I chuckled. "I'm nobody, but New York rocks."

"Someone said you have a boyfriend."

I thought about Richard Ferrara and how to define that relationship. "Boyfriend, no. But I love him."

"So no sex?" Cleve arched his eyebrow, adding, "I get laid here all the time."

"You always get laid," I said. "What about you? Boyfriend?"

Cleve shrugged his shoulders, saying, "Lots of sex, though."

"I don't think I'll ever get married," I said.

"Marriage?" Cleve said. "That'll be the day. We're too crazy. We're scary monsters." Cleve had a way of showing genuine sympathy with a glint of truth's dagger.

The dishwasher kicked in and we sat on the patio and smoked. The stars came out. After we relaxed into familiar comfortable silence, Cleve suddenly said, "I want you to come over more and hang out. I really miss you. You're my best and oldest friend." He got up, pulled me to my feet and hugged me. His eyes glistening, he kissed me quickly like a long-lost brother. "We're the last survivors. We have to stick together."

28

Invisible, with Liberty and Justice for All

Betsy Ross lived in a two-story redbrick row house with white shutters and a shingled pitched roof with a big dormer at 239 Arch Street. It's still there in Philadelphia, and now a museum. I made a pilgrimage to this shrine in 2008.

Betsy Ross was perhaps an invented hero—or heroine. She was always an enigma, never famous in her lifetime, undiscovered until thirty-four years after her death, when her grandson, William J. Canby, recounted her story to the Daughters of the American Revolution in 1870.

Indeed, right after the DAR's discovery of Betsy Ross, her image as an American icon sparked a wave of Gilded Age art. Her likeness was published on everything. She was an allegorical goddess wrapped in red, white, and blue on the sheet music of a John Philip Sousa march. The early suffragists adopted her, giving women a symbolic place in the American pantheon at the centennial of the Revolution.

In the 1950s, she appeared in my grade school history book, wearing a white bonnet, simple blue dress, and shawl. She was depicted as stitching the stars, while George Washington, commander of the Continental Army, resplendent in a gold-buttoned waistcoat, watched by her side. Her myth had been cemented into legend. Essayist and feminist Susan

Sontag called her the consummate artist, still considered relevant two hundred years later.

But when I went to Rome in 2000 for World Pride, no one there had ever heard of Betsy Ross. Her name doesn't mean anything in Europe and the rest of the world. Later, I would learn of Francis Hopkinson, a man credited on his tombstone as the inventor and designer of the American flag. Vexillologists accept his role as a historical fact and are distressed that in the public mind Francis Hopkinson remains anonymous.

Perhaps the legend of Betsy Ross is merely a clever dream, a patriotic illusion, a Victorian projection of nostalgia, a contrived curriculum—a white lie? Even as a doubting iconoclast, I realize that every myth has its truth.

My trip to her house in Philadelphia wasn't a casual visit. Flags are my passion, my craft, and my art. I knew she was an upholstery shop owner, and a woman in business in that era was remarkable. She had three husbands, two of whom died in the Revolutionary War, and seven daughters. A Quaker, she lived most of her long life without access to a sewing machine. It was invented just before she died.

Perhaps George Washington and Francis Hopkinson commissioned her to sew their flag. It's possible, even probable. After all, how many sewing rooms were there in Philadelphia in 1776? I've always given Betsy Ross the benefit of the doubt, paying homage to a fellow seam-master. All flag-makers walk in her long shadow.

The whole colonial facade of her home and the courtyard adjoining it are decked out year-round in cotton buntings. Fans drape from every window and hang end to end along the garden wall. Capping it all off triumphantly, from her dormer window, is an outrigger pole flying a huge American flag. It's a very impressive architectural statement, with a not-so-subliminal marquee announcing this is a secular holy place. Real American history happened here.

You walk in from the street through the courtyard. Reenactors usually perform costumed plays on a little stage under the tree, but there were no actors the day I visited. A crisp red, white, and blue welcome banner hung above the transom of big doors, leading to the gift shop in the small carriage house. That was my first stop.

I looked at the labels on everything to see if it was all made in America. Predictably, few items were. But there were a few homemade tchotchkes on sale from Pennsylvania locals. They sell white bonnets, just like the one Betsy wears in the illustrations. And just like church, there's a collection basket for donations. I felt like I was in Muir Woods, the whole place was so solemn and reverential.

After paying my entry fee to the lady at the counter, I followed her instructions and was led by a docent into the main house, through the back door. It's smaller than it looks. People were tiny then. All the rooms are sealed off with bulletproof Plexiglas, and seemed a little dark for such a sunny day. It turns out hardly anything there is authentic; the few pieces of furniture aren't even hers, though they are from around the same time—disappointing counterfeit relics.

The entire visit was a Disneyland experience. People were guided single file through the narrow, whitewashed hallways, one at a time, up and down the steep, winding staircases. The docent declared dully, "And this is the living room, and this is the bedroom . . ." I glanced through the translucent barriers at the "evidence" of a life reconstructed for tourists, but I wondered what it was really like back then.

People have called me the gay Betsy Ross because I made the Rainbow Flag. As I walked through the house, I tried to summon my illustrious predecessor, hoping for a moment of revelation, a spark of inspiration, a ray of intuition. Nothing happened. Her vibe never reached me, no ghostly visit. Only radio silence.

Maybe I'm jealous of her anonymous and selfless achievement. I send out press releases and film everything I do. Maybe the curtain of technology separates us. My work is so easy and industrial, while hers was one stitch at a time with a needle and hand-spun thread. When I sew flags, I listen to music on loudspeakers. When she did, she heard the sound of horses' hooves on the cobblestones. We do have one true connection: neither of us ever got rich sewing our flags. Across the ages I listened, imagining Betsy living with fearful war, death, and violence all around.

I lingered until the crowds thinned and made my way down to her dim basement workroom, where rusty scissors still hung on a sagging beam. I finally recognized something: a stain on the chunky worn blades, the patina of time revealing the sad color of flags, the invisible warp and weft of hope, courage, blood, and honor. I wondered if the Star-Spangled Banner and the Rainbow Flag are cut from the same cloth.

The fabric of freedom is an open weave, with spaces left for us to insert our own versions of the story. This notion must have crossed Betsy Ross's mind in 1776. The circle of thirteen colonies radiating in her embroidery hoop were a dream of a better world and a new nation, an idea of individual independence and freedom that the Rainbow Flag would disrupt globally centuries later. I wonder if there would even be a Rainbow Flag if it were not for the American flag. Without the American Revolution, would there be a gay rights movement—or any human rights movement at all? Did Betsy Ross see past all the border-lines of nations, race, and gender, sewing the concept of equality, true brotherhood, and sisterhood, in every stitch?

I marveled at her silent modesty. Betsy was only twenty-five when Washington commissioned her handiwork. She lived another fifty years, all the while seeing America grow and, with it, her own creation grow in acceptance and become burnished in legend. I wonder if she made other versions of the flag, adding stars as states were added to the union.

Betsy Ross, wherever you are, your quaint house has been invaded by tourists. They are taking pictures of themselves on cell phones, grabbing brochures that will go unread. They will salute the flag at ball games and parades with lumps of patriotism in their scoundrel throats and think they know you. You've been celebritized for a dumbed-down shorthand understanding of flags.

The painter and sculptor Michelangelo said, "A true work of art is but a shadow of divine perfection." Betsy Ross, your revolutionary act is the ultimate example of the artist as instrument, the hand of God—*invisible*, with liberty and justice for all.

Epilogue

Gilbert Baker's Later Years

by Charley Beal

Manager of Creative Projects, the Gilbert Baker Estate

When Gilbert Baker began writing his memoirs in 1995, he focused the story on his life and his work up through the 1994 creation of the mile-long Rainbow Flag for Stonewall 25. For the most part, subsequent achievements were not chronicled, save for those stand-alone fragments that make up the final two chapters of this book. But Gilbert Baker's life continued on for twenty-three more full and active years. This epilogue acknowledges the additional landmark work by Baker that was not included in his memoir.

After Stonewall 25, Gilbert traveled back and forth between San Francisco and New York, working closely with pioneers in the medical marijuana movement, notably Dennis Peron and Brownie Mary in San Francisco, Dana Beal in New York, and Scott Imler in Los Angeles.

By 1995, Gilbert was working full time for Dennis Peron at the first Cannabis Buyers Club on Market Street. Gilbert convinced Dennis to have every patient using the dispensary present a letter from his or her doctor. Eventually, thousands of patients passed through the doors of the club every week.

In June 1995, Gilbert returned to New York City to carry another giant flag in the annual pride parade down Fifth Avenue. This time, he had legal permission to fly the flag in front of St. Patrick's Cathedral. This tradition would continue for years, eventually replaced by rainbow balloon arches stretching a full city block.

In August 1996, the federal government launched a massive predawn raid on the Cannabis Buyers Club and Dennis Peron's house in San Francisco. Gilbert narrowly escaped arrest but remained in San Francisco, working with activists locally and in Los Angeles. In November 1996, California became the first state to approve medical marijuana use for patients with AIDS and other illnesses.

Gilbert spent the next few years living out of suitcases while working in San Francisco, Los Angeles, and New York.

In San Francisco on November 8, 1997, a Rainbow Flag was installed to fly in perpetuity in Harvey Milk Plaza at the corner of Market and Castro Streets. A bronze plaque at the site identifies Gilbert Baker as the creator of the iconic banner.

In 1998, to mark the twentieth anniversary of the Rainbow Flag, Gilbert re-created the original eight-stripe, hand-dyed banners and raised them again on the original flagpoles at United Nations Plaza in San Francisco. He spent the remainder of the decade in New York with fellow activists, and in Los Angeles working with Scott Imler at the Buyers Club there until the feds closed them down.

In 2000, the year Pope John Paul II celebrated the Great Jubilee to mark the start of the new millennium, Gilbert was invited to mount an art exhibit of his flags and photographs in Rome at the annual World Pride gathering. Because of his controversial history as a Sister of Perpetual Indulgence and Pink Jesus, his planned July exhibition became a target of Vatican officials. Galleries all over Rome were pressured to refuse the exhibition. A venue was finally found—on a barge in the Tiber River—and the art was shipped from the United States. But it was soon impounded at customs. A fundraiser to release the art was organized in New York by Charley Beal and Ann Northrop. The show eventually took place, but after three days it was shut down by authorities. Nonetheless, the World Pride event was a great success; a massive march through Rome included a giant Rainbow Flag.

In 2001, after his reconciliation with Cleve Jones, Gilbert returned to New York and took up permanent residence in a garden apartment on West 150th Street in Harlem's Hamilton Heights. In 2002, he remounted his Rome art show at the LGBT Community Center in New York City. He also contributed artwork for an exhibit at the James C. Hormel Gay and Lesbian Center at the San Francisco Public Library.

In 2003, Gilbert established yet another world record, creating the longest Rainbow Flag in Key West, Florida, for Key West Pride. The 1.25-mile flag was carried the entire length of Key West's Duval Street from the Gulf of Mexico to the Atlantic Ocean to celebrate the twenty-fifth anniversary of the original banner's debut. The event was sponsored by Absolut Vodka, beginning a successful fourteen-year collaboration between Gilbert and the corporate partner. Absolut remained steadfast in its sponsorship of LGBTQ issues in the face of repeated right-wing criticism and boycotts.

For the rest of the decade, Gilbert accepted invitations to serve as grand marshal of pride events in cities around the world. Among the cities that honored him were New York City, Toronto, San Francisco, London, Stockholm, Vancouver, and Winnipeg. Philadelphia's OutFest, the world's largest National Coming Out Day festival, named its annual OutProud award for Gilbert.

In 2008, at the insistence of his friend Cleve Jones, Gilbert returned to San Francisco. He agreed to work on the new Gus Van Sant–directed movie *Milk*, starring Sean Penn in an Oscar-winning performance as the martyred politician. Gilbert re-created period banners for the film and appeared in a cameo role. That year, he expanded his paintings beyond rainbow imagery, creating a series of map paintings in gold bas-relief.

In 2011, Gilbert was honored by the National Gallery of Ireland in Dublin. He presented a Rainbow Flag to Dublin's mayor, Andrew Montague.

In 2012, Gilbert suffered a severe stroke. It affected his peripheral vision and the movement in his left hand. To strengthen his body, he retreated to a house in Cherry Grove on Fire Island and spent the summer in personal rehabilitation therapy: applying beads and sequins by hand to gowns and outfits. In a period of time that surprised doctors, he regained his ability to sew. He reintroduced his drag alter ego of Busty Ross and was crowned "Most Political" at the annual Invasion of the Pines drag event in the neighboring Pines community on July 4.

The accolades increased. San Francisco Pride created the Gilbert Baker Award, presented annually during the festivities in June. In 2015, Gilbert was asked to contribute a Rainbow Flag to the permanent collection at New York City's Museum of Modern Art. The unveiling ceremony took place on June 26, the same day that the US Supreme Court legalized gay marriage nationwide. In the hours that followed, rainbow colors illuminated iconic landmarks throughout the United States, including Niagara Falls, the Empire State Building, One World Trade Center, Cinderella Castle at Walt Disney World, and the White House.

On June 9, 2016, Gilbert attended a White House reception to commemorate LGBT Pride Month. He personally presented President Barack Obama with an original, hand-dyed cotton Rainbow Flag.

In reaction to the election of President Donald Trump in November 2016, Gilbert created a collection of Holocaust-themed outfits emblazoned with pink triangles, the symbol that identified homosexuals in Nazi concentration camps. They were exhibited in a gallery in San Francisco in January 2017. In February, he donated a flag from his thirty-fifth anniversary series to the Design Museum in London. When he suddenly passed away at home in his sleep on March 31, 2017, Gilbert had been planning an April trip back to Parsons, Kansas, where he attended high school. There, he was to be honored at the first annual Gilbert Baker Film Festival at Labette Community College.

Gilbert's legacy: During the New York City memorial service for Gilbert on Flag Day 2017, young activist Luke Camp pays tribute. *Photo by Charley Beal*

Since he began writing his memoirs, Gilbert always planned on publishing them. He enthusiastically shared drafts with a circle of friends, requesting feedback, then made elaborate additions and revisions. At one point, he began shopping his book to publishers. But the reception was cool. Disappointed but not thwarted, Gilbert returned to the material, rewriting and polishing the text extensively. However, activism, art, and his 2012 stroke distracted Gilbert from his writing.

A few months after Gilbert's unexpected death in 2017, I felt it was time to honor my friend's dream of having his memoirs in print. I had a couple of hard copies of the memoir in my possession, and I found other drafts among Gilbert's effects. On his computer's hard drive I found several additional versions of the book, as well as various chapters and fragments, either misplaced, mislabeled, or hidden among other files. I then approached Gilbert's mother, Patricia Baker, and his sister Ardonna Baker Cook and told them that a massive editing job was needed to compile the various drafts into one powerful book. The task was given to Jay Blotcher, a veteran journalist, activist, and editor who was a longtime friend of Gilbert's. Back in 1997, Gilbert had shared the first draft of the memoir with Jay, seeking feedback.

Jay and I formed an editorial team. He trimmed repetitions and then stitched together the disparate versions, based on the best drafts that Gilbert had written. The resulting book, I am confident, offers the best compilation of Gilbert's storytelling of his life.

Acknowledgments

We at the Gilbert Baker Estate would like to acknowledge the following people for their invaluable help in making possible the publication of *Rainbow Warrior: My Life in Color.*

Our deepest thanks are reserved for the people whose energies, blessing, and support allowed this project to go forward: Gilbert's sister Ardonna Baker Cook and his mother, Patricia Baker. To Charley Beal, for spearheading this project from the start and providing unflagging organization, ingenuity, and faith for the long process. To Jay Blotcher, for months of arranging, editing, and reediting numerous drafts of Gilbert's manuscript to produce the final text.

We are grateful for our incredible board of advisers, including Bill Berman, Bruce Cohen, Michelle Fisher, and Matt Foreman, for freely contributing their wisdom and guidance.

For digging into their archives for essential research and photographs, we thank the entire team at San Francisco's GLBT Historical Society: Terry Beswick, Joanna Black, Jeremy Prince, Sean Greene, and Patricia Delara. In Los Angeles, we were ably assisted by Loni Shibuyama and the ONE Archives at the USC Libraries, which allowed us access to their incredible collection of early San Francisco pride parade committee records.

We applaud the many individuals who provided personal recollections and fact-checking as well as moral and physical support during the process: Reginald McKinley, Richard Ferrara, Brook Garrett, Tom Taylor, Dr. Jerome Goldstein, Jude Graham, Cleve Jones, Ann Northrop, and Larry Burnett.

We extend a special thank-you also to our amazingly resourceful literary agent, Robert Guinsler at Sterling Lord Literistic, who tirelessly and passionately carried this project from infancy to publication. To photographers Mick Hicks, Danny Nicoletta, and Mark Rennie, who generously explored their archives to find never-before-seen historical photographs. To Dustin Lance Black for the inspiring foreword. To the Barack Obama Presidential Library for providing the photograph of Gilbert and President Obama. We acknowledge Vincent Guzzone for his endless patience, support, and hours of image editing.

And finally we honor the incredibly talented and committed team at Chicago Review Press: Jerome Pohlen, Andrea Baird, Devon Freeny, and the rest. Their wisdom and patience guided Charley Beal and Jay Blotcher through the challenging but rewarding work that has finally made Gilbert's dream come true: transforming his life story into a book that will illuminate, educate, and inspire.

Selected unpublished fragments from Gilbert's manuscript can be found at www.rainbowwarriorbook.com. Additional information, archival photographs and videos, and breaking news can be found at www.gilbertbaker.com.

The Gilbert Baker Estate is the recipient of all royalties from this memoir.

The mission of the estate is to protect and extend Gilbert Baker's legacy as the creator of the LGBTQ Rainbow Flag, and to honor him as both an activist and an artist.

The estate operates on a collaborative level, working with the LGBTQ community and artists, educational institutions, nonprofits, museums, archives, and the press. The Gilbert Baker Estate is committed to donating all income, after administrative costs, to a number of LGBTQ not-for-profit organizations supported by Gilbert Baker.